My name is Callum Ormond.

I am fifteen

and I am a hunted fugitive . . .

CONSPIRACY 365

BOOK SIX: JUNE

To Robert and Winter

Scholastic Australia
345 Pacific Highway
Lindfield NSW 2070
An imprint of Scholastic Australia Pty Limited
(ABN 11 000 614 577)
PO Box 579
Gosford NSW 2250
www.scholastic.com.au

Part of the Scholastic Group
Sydney • Auckland • New York • Toronto • London
• New Delhi • Hong Kong • Puerto Rico

First published by Scholastic Australia in 2010.

Graphics by Nicole Leary.

Cover design by Natalie Winter.
Cover photography: boy by Wendell Levi Teodoro (www.zeduce.org)
© Scholastic Australia 2010; close-up of boy's face by Michael
Bagnall © Scholastic Australia 2010; jet ski © Joanne Harris
and Daniel Bubnich/Shutterstock; parachuter © Emel Ernalbant/
Shutterstock; cliff © Ana de Sousa/Shutterstock.
Internal photography: paper on page 061 © istockphoto.com/Luseen
Heinlein.

National Library of Australia Cataloguing-in-Publication entry:
Lord, Gabrielle, 1946-
Conspiracy 365: June / Gabrielle Lord.
ISBN 978-1-74169-038-5 (pbk.)
A823.3

ISBN-13:978-93-5103-680-7

Reprinted by Scholastic India Pvt. Ltd., May 2015, 2018

Printed at Shivam Offset Press, New Delhi.

CONSPIRACY 365

BOOK SIX: JUNE

GABRIELLE LORD

SCHOLASTIC
SYDNEY AUCKLAND NEW YORK TORONTO LONDON
NEW DELHI HONG KONG PUERTO RICO

PREVIOUSLY . . .

1 MAY

I'm stuck in Leechwood Lodge Asylum. Sligo's had me admitted under a false identity–Benjamin Galloway–so he can force me to hand over all the documents I have. Truth is, I don't have anything–all of my stuff, including the Riddle, was stolen from my backpack at the boathouse. Dr Snudgeglasser has been completely fooled: convinced I'm delusional, he shrugs off my confession that I am the notorious fugitive, Callum Ormond.

9 MAY

A failed escape attempt puts me in a straitjacket. I'm desperate to get out, but have no idea how to make it happen.

15 MAY

I'm finally allowed out of my cell and into the recreation room, where I see a TV news report about my mum being attacked during a break-in.

While a violent patient goes on a rampage, I sneak unnoticed into an abandoned office. I frantically send an email to Boges, letting him know where I am, begging him to get me out.

19 MAY

The nurse tells me I have visitors. I'm filled with dread as I approach the recreation room, not knowing who or what to expect. Finding Boges and Winter is such a relief. Not only has Boges retrieved my things from the boathouse before it was trashed, but he and Winter have concocted an escape plan. They sneak me out of there . . . dressed in a skirt.

21 MAY

On my way to Great-uncle Bartholomew's I take a risk and hitch another ride. The driver is unhappy about the interference that's suddenly messing with his CB radio. My fake Benjamin Galloway ID saves me from trouble as we pass through a police road block.

Finally I reach 'Kilkenny', but am greeted with threats and a shotgun. After pleading for my great-uncle's help, he puts the gun down and welcomes me in. He shows me the incredible Ormond Orca—the jet he's been building most of his life—and I fill him in on what's been happening.

30 MAY

Old Bartholomew proves to be a great source of information. Our discussions on the Ormond Jewel are interrupted by the arrival of a car near the property—the dark blue Mercedes! We realise I've been bugged—the reason for the radio interference, Oriana's unrelenting ability to track me down, and the constant pain in my right shoulder! Bartholomew digs it out and feeds it to Maggers, his attack-bird companion, who leads the car away on a wild goose chase.

31 MAY

Maggers returns, followed by the Mercedes. While Bartholomew guards the house, I bolt over to a neighbouring property to retrieve important Piers Ormond documents that he says I will find there. After almost being mauled by savage dogs, I break in and grab the papers, but once back at 'Kilkenny' I find my great-uncle on the floor, clutching his chest in pain . . . his bad heart can't take the stress. Sumo and Kelvin set fire to the house and Bartholomew's condition worsens. As the flames intensify, he dies in my arms.

I flee, knowing that my only chance of escape is the Orca. I make it to the jet and take off into the sky. I soar into the night, above the flashing lights of the police at Dimityville Airport below. I try to land, but I crash into the dirt. The Orca skids and twists at unbelievable speeds. When it finally comes to a halt, I find I'm stuck. Smoke begins to fill the cabin . . .

1 JUNE

214 days to go . . .

Big River State Forest

12:00 am

Everything fizzed and flickered out.

The force of the crash-landing had shaken up every cell in my body. I was trembling all over, but my arms and legs felt numb and helpless. I couldn't see a thing—I was surrounded by darkness . . .

Darkness and smoke!

The fumes were filling the cabin, fast. I could feel the small space I was in warming up. My blood pumped, driven by panic. I thrashed my hands around, still trying to find the lever that opened the canopy. I had to get out before I choked to death!

I fumbled around, coughing from the smoke. Something in the undercarriage collapsed, sending the wrecked jet lurching. I fell forward, slamming the windscreen hard with my head. A small crack zigzagged across in front of me, but the thick glass remained otherwise intact.

Then came a *whoomp* from the rear of the aircraft, followed by the crackling of flames—the Orca had fully ignited! Intense heat engulfed me and my desperation soared. I instantly pushed myself back into my seat, brought my knees up and kicked at the canopy with all my power. I kicked again and again until it opened a few centimetres, letting the night air gush in. I gulped it down as the fire behind me intensified.

I kept kicking until finally, I heard a snap. The canopy yielded and I bashed my way out, coughing and spluttering, dragging myself and my backpack out of the cabin.

I rolled to the ground, shot to my feet, and then raced away from the burning wreckage and into the darkness.

12:04 am

After a few seconds I stopped running and looked back. The Ormond Orca was a mass of flames and some nearby trees had caught fire.

As I stood there, mesmerised, watching it all burn in blurry-eyed shock—amazed that I was still alive—the burning Orca buckled, then exploded! The force of the blast was so strong that when it hit me it threw my body to the ground, and I almost collided headfirst with the thick trunk of a tree.

I ducked my head just before a torn panel of the Orca wing hurtled past me and sliced like an axe blade into the tree trunk, just centimetres above me.

12:06 am

From where I was lying, I could see the jet's burning body in the moonlight. Steaming debris was strewn all over the smoky area surrounding what was left of Great-uncle Bartholomew's Orca. If I'd wanted to alert the authorities to where I was, I couldn't have done a better job.

My ears were buzzing and the sound around me was all muffled. I felt around for my backpack, grabbed the strap and pulled it to me. My shoulder throbbed from the bug extraction.

Face-down in the dirt, my damaged body tried to recover and regain control. I couldn't help thinking of Bartholomew and his fighting spirit. It was my fault he was dead. Sumo and Kelvin shouldn't have involved an innocent person, but I shouldn't have either. How much longer could he have lived if I hadn't shown up and brought so much danger with me? He could have had another ten years with his life's work, the Ormond Orca. He spent so long building it—and then it took me just one flight to completely obliterate it all . . . My uncle and his aeroplane crashed on the same day. And they'd both gone up in flames.

'I'm so sorry,' I whispered.

12:13 am

Keeping my head down, I stumbled through the scrubby bushes, trying to get as far away from the wrecked aircraft as I could. My legs weren't obeying me—they were shaky and uneasy, and I kept falling on my hands and knees. I wanted to quit running and find somewhere to hide, but I had to keep going. I knew it wouldn't be long before the crash site would be swarming with the police cars I'd seen from the air. I imagined them racing closer right now, homing in on the smoke billowing in front of the moon like a signal flare.

12:19 am

My exhausted legs suddenly gave out completely from under me, and I fell hard to the ground. I crawled to a sitting position and checked myself over for serious injuries. My fingers were cut and bleeding, my right arm was bruised and had a graze that was slowly seeping blood. Underneath my shredded jeans, my legs were swollen, scratched and bruised.

I dug my phone out and, unbelievably, it was still working. I'd have to get a signal before I could try calling Boges.

I still couldn't believe I'd survived the landing, but I used that piece of luck for motivation to keep walking. Each time I staggered, I got back to my feet and walked on like a crash-test dummy come to life. The sound of distant sirens kicked me back into action and I hobbled deeper into the forest as fast as I could. I wouldn't let them catch me now.

1:35 am

Despite my best efforts I'd been walking pretty slowly, trying to keep close to the edge of the forested area where the moon helped light my path. I was ready to duck back into the dense brush at the slightest alarm. I'd reached a ridge that looked over the lights of a small township in the valley beneath. I figured I could get down there in a couple of hours and decided that as soon as I could find a safe place and a signal, I'd ring Boges. As I stepped over a rocky platform, everything in my vision started fading and melting away . . . all sound dissolved . . . I stumbled, dizzy, and collapsed . . . I held onto my senses just long enough to drag myself under the jutting rock.

6:45 am

My eyes opened and I bumped my head on the rock that I'd forgotten was above me. My body was half undercover, half exposed—I must have blacked out, exhausted. I shivered and pulled myself up in a tight ball to get warm.

Sunlight was starting to streak across the sky and, in the east, the horizon was a light grey. It was time to get going. Stiff and sore with cold, I got up and started walking down the sloping ground, sliding and slithering, heading for the town I'd seen last night.

I must have been about halfway down, and had reached a wide, level clearing when I heard voices. I stopped, ducked back behind a eucalyptus tree, and kept completely still, listening intently.

'. . . can't have gone too far . . . somewhere around here . . . Joe McAlister said he thought he saw someone heading east from the crash scene.'

The man's voice got louder as it came closer to my pitiful hiding place.

'He's had all night to make his escape,' said another male voice. 'He could be anywhere by now.'

'You saw the plane wreck,' the first voice continued. 'It's a miracle he walked away from that, so I reckon he's gotta be pretty messed up. Probably got some serious injuries. I don't reckon he could've got very far.'

I crouched down, grabbing the straps of my backpack tightly, nervously making myself as small as possible.

'Cover this area thoroughly. I'm going to head that way. Meet you back at Stony Falls Creek Road.'

The first voice seemed to trail off, so I figured I only had one searcher to deal with.

Seconds later, footsteps approached the eucalypt I was crouched behind. They cautiously trudged through the damp, fallen leaves, and for a second my mind flashed back to the painstaking moments I'd spent hiding in the rocky crevice after fleeing the Blackwattle Creek car crash.

But this time I knew that whoever was approaching was more than likely going to see me. I needed to decide, fast, whether I should run, or stay and fight.

I'd hesitated too much to run, and began bracing myself for an attack when I felt something strange—some sort of vibration—under my feet. The ground was rumbling! The trees around me were bending, and leaves were lashing, as a powerful wind whipped my face. I knew this sound, I knew this feeling . . . I looked up, and there in the sky was a helicopter descending!

I squinted, trying to get a better look at it. It was black and sleek, smaller than the ones I'd seen before. It didn't look like a police chopper, so who was the pilot?

I glanced around, trying to locate the guy who'd almost been on me moments ago. He was just metres away, cowering and shielding himself from the windy blast, his light brown overcoat flapping behind him. I wanted to run while he was distracted, but my only path was through the clearing, and that was impossible right now. Instead, I retreated, and watched as the helicopter descended in a cloud of dust, now only metres from the ground.

To my horror, I saw two familiar figures climb out of the cabin and creep along the skids. One after the other, they jumped to the ground.

Sumo and Kelvin!

The helicopter lifted and thundered back into the sky, quickly disappearing from sight as Sumo and Kelvin straightened up and started scanning the place. The guy in the coat approached them.

I was trapped: I couldn't backtrack, and I had nowhere to run, except right for them!

Then came a sound from behind me like drumming. It approached, becoming louder and louder, like a wayward train. This was no helicopter, but whatever it was had distracted the three guys in my view.

'What's going on?' I heard one of them shout.

The noise was thunderous. I turned around and through the scrub, I saw dusty flashes of movement, then a blur of dashing legs and tossing heads—a mob of wild brumbies! They must have been disturbed by the chopper! Down through the trees they galloped as a group, deftly jumping over logs, kicking up dirt and startling birds that rose squawking at their passing. They were coming right for us—we would be run down, trampled! Smashed to pieces by sharp hooves!

I grabbed the trunk of the tree beside me and pulled myself as close to it as possible. I had no choice but to close my eyes and hope for the best as the mob dashed my way. The pounding closed in and the entire mob rushed at me in a deafening haze of reckless hooves.

The thud of their hooves finally faded and all was still again. I crouched next to the eucalyptus tree, listening. All I could hear was the silence of the forest. They were gone. I was unscathed! I wiped dirt from my face and looked into the clearing. As the dust settled I saw a writhing body laying in the path the brumbies had taken. It was Kelvin! He'd been trampled!

Sumo and the other guy ran to his side. This was my chance! I sucked up the pain in my aching body and ran for it.

9:29 am

I'd almost reached the town, so I stopped in a secluded, sheltered spot to try to clean myself up a bit. I could feel blood caked on my forehead and my knuckles, and my jeans were tattered and torn—obviously they were not designed to withstand vicious dog attacks, plane crashes, or fugitive runs through the bush.

From the bottom of my backpack, I gratefully dug out the tracksuit Melba had given me, and awkwardly pulled it on. The warm, fleecy material was comforting, and it kept the icy morning air at bay. I made the best of my appearance and tentatively walked into a potential trap waiting for me in town.

Big River

9:37 am

Big River was a medium-sized country town, and from where I stood it looked like most of its shops were closed. One had its doors open—a small convenience store, with faded green strips of plastic dangling over the doorway. I couldn't see anyone suspicious—no cops, no park rangers, and no sign of Oriana's thugs. There was no-one around at all, aside from an old blue cattle dog tied to a wooden bench out the front of the open store. I went over and scanned the ads and signs in the shop window for what I was looking for, and there it was: a crooked, handwritten poster that read, 'High Speed Internet'.

I huddled down beside a post office box and called Boges.

'Cal,' he said a bit sleepily, 'are you OK? I heard something about arson, murder and theft. Sounds like my friend Cal, I thought. What happened?'

'I'm all right, but Great-uncle Bartholomew died right in front of me. He had a heart attack,' I said. 'Sumo and Kelvin showed up, then they set the house alight . . . and he pretty much died right there in my arms. If it weren't for me, he'd still be alive.'

'That's rough, dude. But not your fault, OK?' Boges said slowly, urging me to agree with him. 'Your uncle was really old, right? And probably not in the best shape already. Don't beat yourself up about it.'

'Hard not to,' I said, knowing what Boges was saying was true, but also knowing that my search for clues to the Ormond Singularity had impacted badly on another innocent person. 'They were smoking us out of the house,' I continued, 'and I had to get away from there, so I . . .'

'So you?'

'So I took the jet.'

'You what?!' Boges screeched.

'I wouldn't have stood a chance on foot, and before he died, Bartholomew told me to take the Orca. So that's what I did.'

'Incredible!'

'It was awesome! I was absolutely freaking out, but it flew and it got me out of there. I landed near Dimityville Airport. Well, I crash-landed. Just got out before the whole thing exploded.'

'Are you serious?!'

'Deadly. I can't believe it myself. Sumo and Kelvin nearly got me again earlier this morning, but anyway . . . I've just reached a town called Big River, and there's a place I can see that looks like it has internet connection,' I said, thinking of all the sensitive information I wanted to pass on to Boges.

'Discretion,' he said, understanding.

'That's right.'

'Chat online? I can text you new login details.'

'Yep,' I agreed. 'I'll be online in ten.'

'Cool, but be careful there's no-one hanging around, searching for you. I'm sure the cops are crawling over the place, and don't forget you have the private detective your uncle Rafe hired on your case, too.'

'Yep. It seems OK right now, but I don't want to stick around for long. I need to go and find a new place to hide out for a while.'

9:47 am

I hurried over and peered into the shop. In the back, behind shelves stacked with tinned food and jars, were two old, bulky computers sitting side by side on a desk with orange plastic chairs in front of them.

I parted the plastic strips and walked through the doorway. The woman behind the counter took no notice of me, barely looking at me as I bought a packet of chips, a muffin and a bottle of orange juice. She was glued to a small TV that was propped up near the register on some phone books. The place was quiet except for the sound of the TV chattering away with some talk-show hosts dishing out bad jokes and cheesy smiles in between infomercials.

'I want to log on, too,' I said.

She shrugged, sniffing and giving me my change. 'Either of those,' she said, pointing to the back of the shop.

9:52 am

I sat down at the first stone-age computer, glancing back towards the street. Still no-one around. I signed-in to chat, all the time automatically scanning the street outside the doorway. I hoped the brumby incident had taken Kelvin, at least, off my back for now, but Sumo could still be in hot pursuit, and the police would be scouring the townships surrounding Dimityville.

A news banner stretching across the top of the monitor caught my attention. I clicked on the featured photo that I instantly recognised as being 'Kilkenny'. A video clip slowly loaded and soon I was watching aerial footage of police and firemen surrounding the smouldering ashes of the house.

I sat there in a trance, remembering all that had happened at that place. Sadness welled up in me as I thought of my old great-uncle. A newsreader interrupted the footage to bring the latest on the story, while images of the

Ormond Orca crash site replaced the Mount Helicon home. I leaned in so I could listen to it on low volume.

'The wreck of the stolen jet—belonging to the elderly Mount Helicon resident Bartholomew Ormond, who earlier perished in a deliberately-lit fire following a home invasion—has been located in Big River State Forest,' reported the newsreader. 'Police have not retrieved a body from the crash site. An internal source has reported that the offender is none other than 15-year-old Callum Ormond, and that he may be seriously injured. Callum, the victim's nephew, is the teen fugitive whom police have been seeking for many months. He is considered to be armed and extremely dangerous. The public are being warned against approaching him. Police are appealing for information on his whereabouts. It's alleged Callum lit the fire deliberately to cover the theft of the aircraft, and the murder of Bartholomew Ormond.'

9:56 am

---

login name: dmo_hunter. password: bogesisawesome. i'll be on in 5.

I killed time waiting for Boges by jumping onto my blog and typing up a new message.

Web | Images | Video | News | Maps | More

Web Search

Hello, Callum

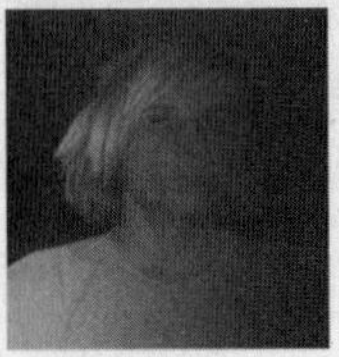

Contact Cal

Messages for Cal

Male
15 years old
Richmond

Please don't believe the latest reports that are going down right now about how I killed an old man, set fire to his house and stole his aeroplane. It's all lies. Don't ask me how the cops are getting it so wrong. It all feels like a conspiracy. Yes, I went to 'Kilkenny'. I went there to see if my great-uncle could help me out of this mess. These two guys who've been chasing me for months turned up at his property. They set fire to the house to get me out of there. But it wasn't me or the fire that killed Bartholomew . . . it was the stress of it all. We were under attack and his heart couldn't take it. I never meant for him to get caught up in this nightmare. I only wanted his help. And he died trying to protect his home . . . and me.

My great-uncle told me to fly the jet—the Ormond Orca. He spent his whole life crafting it, and he wanted me to use it to fly myself out of danger.

Here is the truth: murderous criminal gangs are constantly threatening my life and I have been forced to take drastic action to save myself. Every single thing I've done has been about protecting my family and staying alive. I've only ever acted in self-defence and would never intentionally hurt anybody.

Oriana de la Force is behind my great-uncle's death. The police should investigate her.

Inbox [1]
Update Profile
Sign Out

POSTED BY TEENFUGITIVE AT 10:01 AM

1 Messages

bogesy: u there?

dmo_hunter: yep, thanks for sorting that out. just saw a newsflash from kilkenny. cops r blaming me . . . as usual. calling me a murderer. again.

bogesy: yeah, i saw it too. do what u can to ignore it. gran's just calling out. back in a minute.

Next I checked some of the new comments on my wall. Lots were from people whose names were becoming familiar, like Jas and Tash. Seeing all the friendly comments from people who believed in me really made me feel a whole lot better. But I was missing home real bad . . . and I knew all the friendly messages in the world couldn't stop a question coming into my mind, no matter how hard I tried to push it away: how come total strangers believed in me when my own mother didn't?

10:11 am

dmo_hunter: back yet?

Boges hadn't returned. I was starting to get frustrated and twitchy in my plastic seat, when I realised I had a private message waiting for me on my blog. It was a message from a stranger.

Web | Images | Video | News | Maps | More

Web Search

Hello, Callum

Contact Cal

Messages for Cal

Inbox | Sent | Drafts

From: N.Sharkey

Hello Cal,

I'm an ex-police detective who has been following your case with great interest. I know what it's like to be wrongly accused and from what I can see and read, I'm inclined to believe in your innocence.

If there is anything I can do to help—I should tell you I don't have a lot of money so I can't help in any official way—please let me know if you are interested and I will do my best.

Sincerely, Nelson Sharkey
Mobile: 0341 052 132

I read the email a few times over. Was Nelson Sharkey genuine or were the police trying a new tack, hoping to trick me into contacting them and revealing my position? There was something about the message that rang true. Or maybe I just wanted it to. I was suspicious. Life on the run had made me a totally different person from the trusting kid I'd once been.

I didn't reply to the email but made a note of the phone number Nelson Sharkey left and then went back to check on Boges again.

dmo_hunter: you back? prob not a great idea for me to hang out in here too much longer.

bogesy: sorry dude, gran just spilled a carton of milk all over the kitchen floor, and she couldn't bend over to clean it up. bad back. she was trying to mop it up with two tea towels under her feet . . .

dmo_hunter: lol.

bogesy: yeah, pretty funny. before u ask, gab's ok. still on life support, still no real change, but no more talk of switching her off. rafe's the same as always, and your mum's pretty much the same too. and by 'the same' i mean 'weird'.

I recalled the scene with Mum at the hospital and felt my muscles tense with anger. I still hadn't forgiven her. I filed that thought away and forced my attention back to Boges.

dmo_hunter: soon as I can, i'll be back in town.

bogesy: only if it's safe.

dmo_hunter: i just read an email from an ex-cop, a guy called nelson sharkey. it came in through my blog. he said he wants to help me. reckons he knows what it's like to be falsely accused of something. said he believes i'm innocent and that i could contact him if i wanted his help.

bogesy: . . .

dmo_hunter: i'm not stupid, i'm not about to write back and arrange a meeting. i know it's probably a set-up.

bogesy: i didn't say u were stupid. it's just . . . so hard to know who to trust. but u never know, he could be legit. it's about time you got a good break. an ex-detective on our side could be very helpful. don't make any hasty decisions on that one. hey, explain 'magpie'?

dmo_hunter: magpie. ok. oriana bugged me. buried a transmitter in my shoulder, back when she abducted me in january.

bogesy: what?! she's been able to track you all along?!!

dmo_hunter: i know! anyway, when we realised it was there, bartholomew dug it out for me and then he fed it to his pet magpie, along with some mince or something, so that the bird would lead oriana's thugs away from where we really were. worked for a day or so . . . until maggers came back.

bogesy: so cool.

dmo_hunter: my great-uncle was awesome. we also talked about the ormond jewel and I reckon my dad might have used our life savings to buy it from someone. remember how all our money disappeared? one hundred thousand dollars? the ormond jewel had been given to an ancestor in tudor times by queen elizabeth 1 herself.

bogesy: awesome! that's why there was the empty jewel case and that's why your place was broken into! but who's your ancestor?

dmo_hunter: a guy called black tom butler, the tenth earl of ormond. he was an agent of the queen in ireland.

bogesy: dude, the *black*jack! black tom! that's what the drawing must have meant! and . . . it's a butler with the tray, not a waiter! like winter said.

dmo_hunter: exactly! black tom was a rich and powerful earl back in the days of QE1, and looked after her interests in ireland. i think that's why she gave BT the jewel, like a bonus or something.

bogesy: we need to track this down—fast! so what does it look like?

dmo_hunter: like a giant emerald, set in gold with rubies and pearls around it. and it's a locket that opens up to a miniature portrait of QE1.

bogesy: nice, nice.

dmo_hunter: hope so. u seen winter lately?

bogesy: not since we sprang you from the clinic. she rang me that night and told me she got out ok. why?

dmo_hunter: no reason.

bogesy: all this new info is going to make our investigation heaps easier.

dmo_hunter: doesn't feel like it's getting easier. we're dealing with a double-key code. great-uncle bart told me that the ormond riddle and the ormond jewel had to be put together somehow to solve the mystery of the huge secret my dad had stumbled on in ireland—the ormond singularity. we're almost halfway through the year, and we have a long way to go yet.

bogesy: we'll get there.

dmo_hunter: how the heck are we going to figure out the ormond singularity? we don't have a clue where the jewel is, and the riddle has the last two lines cut off! HOW ARE WE EVER GOING TO FIND THEM AND BRING THEM TOGETHER?

bogesy: we'll get there. somehow.

dmo_hunter: if you say so. another thing, my great-uncle told me i should speak to his sister, my great-aunt millicent. he reckoned she could have access to helpful info.

bogesy: he's right, you should speak to her. where is she?

dmo_hunter: i don't have a clue. we've never met. i'd almost forgotten all about her. and it's too late to ask bartholomew for more details.

bogesy: i'll see what I can do. hey, i have something for you.

dmo_hunter: ?

bogesy: jennifer smith's number. i'll text it to you.

dmo_hunter: you're a legend. back in touch soon, ok.

10:41 am

I was about to get up and leave, thinking if there was still no-one around I'd get onto the highway and try my luck getting a lift back to the city, when a guy came into the shop to buy milk.

'What's going on round this place?' he asked the woman at the cash register, who stared back blankly at him. 'There's roadblocks in and out of town,' he explained. 'You got an escaped criminal on the loose round here?'

The woman shrugged. 'I dunno,' she said. 'I don't listen to the news. It's all bad.'

'Come on,' said the man, picking up his milk and his change, 'you ought to look on the bright side.'

The girl looked around the convenience store. 'Not much of that round here,' she muttered.

It was so frustrating being delayed again, when I had so many leads I wanted to look into, but it was clear I needed to keep out of sight for a while, until the roadblocks were lifted—make the authorities believe I'd left the area.

When the man walked out of the store, I paid for my internet usage, bought a loaf of bread, some peanut butter and another bottle of juice and moved on.

Keeping away from the shops that had just started to come alive with customers, I followed signs to a picnic ground. It was a grassy area where wintering willow trees hung over a brown river. It made me think of a place Mum and Dad took me and Gabbi to a couple of summers ago to learn how to jet ski. There was a small toilet block, and a brick barbecue and wooden table with benches were set out near a narrow white footbridge that led to the other side of the river. The place was deserted. It wasn't the season or the time for picnics.

After ducking into the toilets, I hurried over the footbridge, noticing a low, isolated building set several hundred metres upriver. It looked like a scout hall or some kind of community building–it had a padlocked double door at one end, and a row of web-covered windows along the river side. A faded notice outside the door indicated that it was a summer camp for visiting scout groups, but could be used in the winter for other community meetings.

A broken window at the far end of the building was exactly the sort of thing I was looking for, and it didn't take me long to get through it and inside. I found myself in a small room with two sets of bunk beds on either side. Opposite that room was another one, completely identical. There were three sets of these rooms in a line, enough beds for twenty-four people. Further along was a bathroom, a run-down kitchen, a storage area, and the hall, which had a raised area like a stage at the front, next to a lectern.

I grabbed a sleeping-bag from a pile in the storage area and dragged it along with me, thinking I'd take it with me when I left. The interior was cold but I was exhausted. I went back to the room opposite the one I had first come into, and flicked on the lamp that was sitting on the bedside table. It worked; light filled the room. I pulled the plug out and stuck my phone charger in instead, then threw myself on one of the lower bunks and pulled a folded blanket over me.

Images of Great-uncle Bartholomew's pale face as he lay dying on the floor by his telescope wouldn't leave my mind. At least we had some time together, I told myself. And without that, I might never have known about the existence of the Ormond Jewel, or Black Tom Butler, or found the potential leads on the Ormond Singularity . . . which was ticking down to extinction with every passing day.

I knew I had to shake off these disturbing thoughts and get some sleep.

2 JUNE

213 days to go . . .

Waratah Scout Hall

9:25 am

I snuck out of the hall and ventured back over the footbridge to town to suss out the roadblock and police presence situation. I didn't quite make it to the roadblocks—the local buzz was enough to send me right back into hiding. Out of sight in the bush behind the main strip of shops I overheard a few locals talking about me, and it seemed like the possibility of Callum Ormond, 'Psycho Kid', passing through Big River was probably the most exciting thing that had ever happened in this town.

On the long way back to the footbridge—sticking to the cover of the trees—I spotted train tracks that led me to a small platform at the local railway station. It was deserted, but I hoped it still had the odd train coming through, so I could use it to get out of here if I needed to.

11:27 am

Safely back at the scout hall, I sat cross-legged on my bunk bed, eating a sandwich I'd made and planning the next couple of days. It was hard—my brain felt really fuzzy, as I hadn't slept well at all.

There were a few things I could get done while I was stuck here. I needed to contact my dad's colleague, Eric Blair, and I really needed to talk to Jennifer Smith. Now that I had her number again I wanted to find out how I could get my hands on the memory stick that contained Dad's photos from Ireland.

12:02 pm

'Eric Blair, please.'

'Eric's on leave, can I pass your call on to Wayne Slattery?' the receptionist replied, in an impatient monotone.

Still? What was wrong with him?

'No thanks, that won't be necessary,' I replied, frustrated. 'Will Eric be returning to the office any time soon?'

'Eric won't . . .' the receptionist's voice trailed off for a moment. 'You've called here before, haven't you?' she asked. 'Can I take your name and number and have someone call you?'

'Er, no, that's fine,' I mumbled before hanging

up, completely confused.

I couldn't remember when I'd first called Dad's old work to speak to Eric, but I was fairly sure he'd been 'off sick' or 'on leave' for months. His mysterious absence had gone on for too long. Something was up. He was the one guy I knew that had been in Ireland when Dad got sick. What if they'd both contracted the UVI– the unknown viral infection? I needed to find out what his story was, and I had so few leads; I needed all the information there was. Somehow I'd need to find another way to get to him.

12:33 pm

'Hi, it's Cal,' I said, when Jennifer answered her phone.

'Cal! Where are you? How are you?' Her warm, friendly voice sounded genuinely concerned. 'I'm so happy to hear from you! I've been trying to call you but your phone was disconnected.'

'Yep, I lost that one,' I said, picturing it sitting in a drawer somewhere in Leechwood Lodge. 'I have another one now.'

'You're OK?'

'I'm cool,' I said, looking around at the dusty scout cabin I was sitting in. 'I'm sure you've heard plenty of what I've been up to. The cops' version, at least. I went to my great-uncle in

Mount Helicon, hoping he'd be able to help me, but the visit was cut short . . . he had a heart attack, and I was chased out of there. But, anyway . . . I'm ringing about the memory stick.'

'Yes, of course. I've been wondering how to get it to you. I'm so sorry to hear about your uncle. I saw reports of the fire on the news. The jet crash too—they said there wasn't a body in the wreckage, and that you'd walked away from it. I was praying that was true. I'm so relieved to hear your voice,' she said with a huge exhale.

'Thank you,' I said. It was so good to feel that concern from her—someone who actually believed in me and wanted to help, rather than hunt me down and hand me in. It was what had been so great about being with Bartholomew, too, even if only for a short time. It also reminded me of what I was missing from my mum.

'I'm fine,' I managed to say through the lump in my throat. 'I've got some cuts and bruises, but nothing to worry about. Jennifer,' I said, getting back to my dad's photos, 'I was wondering if you could please send that memory stick to a friend's address?'

'Will it be safe?'

'I think so,' I said, before giving her Boges's address.

'I'll register it,' she said, taking down the

details. 'An extra bit of caution can't hurt. If I make the post in time, I'll send it out today. If not, tomorrow morning.'

'Thanks so much. I can't wait to see what's on there.'

'I just hope it reaches you OK. Cal, I really admire you and what you're doing,' she added.

'I'm just doing what I can,' I said, 'to survive.'

'I think you're doing a lot more than that. I've worked with heaps of different people who've found themselves in bad circumstances. It's only when things are really tough that the true character of people shows through. It's easy to be good-hearted when everything's going well, not so easy otherwise. None of us can completely control what happens in our lives, but we can choose how we react to them. You should be proud of yourself. I just wish I could be of more help to you.'

'You have been a huge help already,' I said. 'Thanks. I'll keep in touch, OK.'

3 JUNE

212 days to go . . .

10:12 pm

Another whole day gone in the scout hall . . . Another sleepless night ahead . . .

I'd snuck out again to suss out whether the buzz had died down in town, and the locals already seemed to have adjusted to being encircled by authorities. It's amazing how quickly people can adapt to new circumstances, I thought to myself. I felt like I was still fighting my life on the run—I refused to accept it. I had to keep believing that getting back my old life was possible.

I'd still spent all day being really paranoid that a search team would show up, or even a group of school kids or an old ladies' knitting class. I'd been heaps edgy, ready to grab my stuff and leap out the window at the first hint of a threat. I was trying to do something useful before it was cool for me to move on, but it was so difficult to relax and look over all my stuff, hoping for breakthroughs, when I couldn't stop checking the windows for intruders.

Whenever I started feeling really trapped, I closed my eyes and imagined being back in my cell at Leechwood. Being here was nothing like that.

4 JUNE

211 days to go . . .

6:02 am

My heart was racing, pounding in my chest! Something was terribly wrong. I was in danger. I didn't know where I was. Floating towards me was the threadbare white toy dog, and behind it was a crying baby. I wanted to scream as the dog came closer and the baby's cries got louder, but no sound would come out of my mouth.

I sat up, panting, clutching the blanket around me. I'd just woken up from the nightmare again, feeling more than ever how familiar the toy dog was. Was it just because I'd seen it in my dreams so many times?

I sat up shivering for a long time. I'd been so anxious last night that it was no wonder the nightmare had returned. I could hardly recall what it was like to have a relaxing, restful sleep. Eventually I calmed down and tried to get some shut-eye.

10:05 am

Something outside woke me up and I scrambled out of bed on instant alert. A few car doors slammed, while voices drifted into the hall from two directions. Someone was loudly fumbling with the front door down the other end of the building, and even though it was a dark and cloudy morning, I could see a cop car parked next to a ranger's Jeep through the broken window. A woman in khaki—the park ranger—was out there talking to one of the cops. Both my exits were covered. I was trapped!

The front door rattled—they'd have it open in seconds! I started shoving all my stuff under the bed. My backpack, the drawings, my phone. I straightened the sheets and the blanket from where I'd been sleeping. I ran to the bathroom and grabbed the clothes I'd left there on the floor last night, then ran back to the bed and tossed them under with everything else.

As the front door creaked open and light flooded in, I launched myself under another bunk, squeezing as far back as I could possibly go.

I could hardly breathe as two or three people with torches entered the scout hall, scanning the premises. I pulled my legs up, afraid they might be spotted sticking out from under the bottom of the bed, and started running a mental check of all my things. Had I left anything incriminating lying somewhere? It was too late now.

My phone charger! I reached out and grabbed the cord, ripped it out of the wall, and snatched it towards me, out of sight.

'What was that?' one of the voices asked.

'I didn't hear anything,' another replied. 'But who knows what kind of animals could be lurking in here.'

Light and shadows shifted as they approached with their torches. The sound of curtains being pulled, and doors being kicked open and closed, echoed down the hallway. Any second now and they'd be metres from me.

I tried to hold my breath as I watched three pairs of muddy, black leather boots tread into the room, closer and closer to where I was hidden. Beams of torchlight traced the beds while I silently begged I'd go unseen.

'What's that?' said a voice, as boots stepped mere centimetres from where my face was trembling under the bed. A torch drew a slow line of light across the floor and stopped on something small and glinting.

My guardian angel pin! It must have fallen off when I was grabbing everything up!

A big, tanned hand reached down and picked

up the angel. There was a moment of silence before someone spoke again.

'Ah, it's nothing. Just a pin some kid must have left behind here in summer. Let's go.' The boots began leaving the room. 'Waratah's clear,' he spoke into a crackling walkie talkie. 'Has someone checked the primary school or the old bakehouse?'

The last guy awaited instruction in the doorway. *Please leave*, I urged.

'OK, we'll go there next,' he said, and walked away.

I waited, completely still, under the bed until I heard both cars drive away from the hall. When I finally emerged, I breathed a massive sigh of relief and smiled at the guardian angel pin, left sitting on the bedside table.

5 JUNE

210 days to go . . .

8:41 am

I wasn't sure if I could take another day of waiting in the scout hall for someone to spring me. I figured I'd used up all my luck in Big River yesterday, hiding from the cops, and was trying to decide my next move when I heard a car pull up on the dirt outside.

My mind jumped straight to the cops again, but through the window I saw two little girls in matching pink leotards hop out of a maroon four-wheel drive. Next, a woman, carrying sparkly bags and an MP3 player hopped out from the driver's seat.

Then another car loaded up with more giggling girls pulled up.

It was time to go! I'd been booted out by a class of ballerinas!

I shoved everything into my backpack, grabbed the sleeping-bag I'd pinched from the storage room, neatened up the bed I'd been sleeping on, and slid back out the window I'd originally come through.

9:30 am

After a cold walk through the frosty grass along the riverbank, I made my way to the station on the outskirts of town that I'd found a couple of days ago. A few people had gathered on the platform, so I took a pretty big risk and bought a ticket with my Ben Galloway travel pass, and jumped on the first train that pulled in. It was travelling along the coast, heading back to the city. I was relieved that nobody took any notice of me.

I was so keen to get back to the city, see Boges, and pick up where we'd left off. Part of me was also keen to get back there because it was where Winter lived. I wanted to see her again—I was hoping she still wanted to help me and Boges work everything out.

My next problem was finding somewhere new to stay—some place where I could lie low for a while, get together with Boges and Winter and keep trying to make sense of the new information I had. I was counting on Jennifer having posted Boges the memory stick, which I hoped would reveal something to help us understand the Ormond Singularity or the double-key code. Also, now that we knew about its existence, we needed to get as much information as possible on the Ormond Jewel and its location.

As I sat in an empty carriage of the train, watching the coastal scenery speed past the windows of the train, I kept thinking of home. Being with Great-uncle Bartholomew was the closest I'd felt to it in a long time. He was cool. I felt like I'd known him my whole life. His face, filled with worry for me as he lay dying, drifted into my mind again. My stomach churned and I felt sick with guilt and sadness. The countryside I was staring at through the train window blurred.

Central Station

12:20 pm

Pulling my hoodie tighter around my face, I got off the train and blended in with the rest of the passengers heading for the exit ramp.

My heart started racing when I saw a couple of cops at the ticket barriers, randomly checking the IDs of people about my age. I could see their eyes scanning everyone coming up from the train. I saw the young policewoman's eyes focus on me and narrow, and I felt like guilt was written all over my face. I had no choice but to keep moving forward. I inched towards the potential catastrophe. If they caught me now, I'd never work things out . . . or see Winter again.

'You,' she said, calling me aside, like I expected. 'Got any ID?'

I fumbled nervously in the pocket of my hoodie and finally brought out Ben Galloway's travel pass. The police officer's partner wasn't taking any notice of me. He was too busy checking out the rest of the possibilities, but the one in front of me was sure giving me the once over.

'How did you get that bruise?' she said, looking closely at my face.

'Softball. Well, not-so-soft-ball,' I laughed, remembering something that had happened to Boges a few years ago. 'At school. My friend smashed the ball, and I copped it right in the face,' I said, amazed at how convincing I sounded.

I could see her running a lot of programs behind her eyes. Then slowly I saw her decide to let me go.

'OK,' she said, passing the ID back to me. 'Pay more attention next time—gotta keep your eye on the ball. On your way.'

I could feel her watching me as I walked away, fighting the desire to break into a run. I caught a glimpse of my reflection in the window of a passing train, and I realised why she'd stopped me and studied me so hard. Even though I'd scrubbed up while I was staying at the scout hall, and I was wearing clothes that looked half decent, up close I worried I looked like a guy you'd cross the street to avoid. I guessed I looked like trouble.

And I'd had plenty of trouble. I'd been in so many deadly situations since I'd heard about the Ormond Singularity. They flashed into my mind as I made my way out of the station. Despite a violent storm at sea and being targeted by sharks, I'd managed to escape. I had been miraculously saved from the screeching train when I was stuck on the railway line, and I'd managed to walk away from the crash-landing of a jet. I'd been abducted, I'd been hunted, and yet I was still free. How much longer could I stay that way? Could I really make it through all three hundred and sixty-five days?

12:42 pm

'Dude! You're back in town,' said Boges. I'd called him the second I'd made it to a quiet spot far enough away from the station and prying eyes. 'Where are you?'

'I just got off at Central Station—used the Ben

Galloway ID. Now I'm looking for somewhere to stay. There's no way I can go back to the boat-house. It's not safe there any more. I'm out of ideas.'

'Your best buddy might have a solution to your housing problem!'

'Really?'

'Yep. One of my cousins just bought a block of land and guess what? There's a caravan still parked on it. I checked it out. It's kind of old, but liveable—if you don't mind a water feature when it rains.'

'It leaks, huh?'

'Sure does. But it's better than nothing, and it's in a quiet spot. My cousin won't be cleaning up the lot for a couple of months—he's away at the moment—so I reckon it's perfect for you. It's about four kilometres from school. You know where the old bus terminus used to be? It's not far from there. Can you meet me there at four?'

'Cool, see you then.'

2:55 pm

I walked towards the bus terminus, where I was meeting Boges, but kept my distance from school. I didn't want to bump into anyone who might recognise me.

The old bus terminus was nothing much

more than a turnaround area and some broken-down sheds. A fading, water-damaged real estate billboard showed the fancy apartment block that was supposed to be going up there ages ago. But nothing had happened there for years.

3:59 pm

Boges turned up with a big bag of stuff that he hoisted off his shoulder as he approached me.

'Man, look at you!'

'This is what happens when you get bugged, chased, debugged, almost torn to pieces by crazy dogs, caught in a house fire, watch a man die, take off and crash-land an experimental jet, try to escape through the forest, spend a few days hiding out in a scout hall . . . Just your average holiday in the country.'

Boges laughed, but after his wide grin, his face was quickly serious. 'You've sure been through hell, dude. Come on, it's not far now. Here's your chance to rest up a bit and recharge, OK? I want my best mate to stay alive!'

We walked for a few minutes until we came to an almost-vacant block of land, overgrown with long grass and with a padlocked gate across a newish driveway. Trees and shrubs ran around three sides of the block, protecting it from the gaze of curious neighbours. Boges glanced around before unlocking the gate and leading me to the only sign of habitation—the old caravan down the other end of the block.

'I know it looks like it was last used by the early explorers,' said Boges. 'And maybe it was! But you can call it home. At least until I tell you otherwise.'

'Ha!' I said, as we approached the old van. 'I've slept in far worse places than this. This will be like my own little piece of paradise.'

I stepped up to the front door, which was already slightly ajar, and pushed it open, ducking my head a little to step inside. It smelled damp and a bit mouldy and I could see tree leaves growing through a large hole in one end of the roof. A bunk bed ran down one side and a small, fold-out table and bench seat ran along the other. A rusty hot plate and a few small cupboards above this completed the furnishings.

'Not bad,' I said, looking around and gratefully dumping my backpack onto the lower bunk. 'It'll do just fine.'

Boges emptied his bag beside my backpack. He'd brought me a bunch of stuff, including heaps of food, some drinks and some more clothes.

'There's no power here,' he said, 'or a functional toilet, but I've got new batteries, a spare battery for your phone, another torch . . .

and some,' he paused to pull out something else from the bottom of his bag, 'toilet paper! Also, the water tank is filled, so you can use the tap.' He turned on the tap in the little sink. 'But go easy on it. And don't draw too much attention to yourself,' he said. 'The neighbours can't really see in here, and they're used to my cousin using the van sometimes, like when he started building the driveway.'

'Thanks for all this,' I said, sorting through everything he'd emptied out on the bed.

'I've put it on the bill, dude. I gotta go. I've got a shocker assignment due. Shakespeare. Not really my area of interest. Give me algebra and complex equations any day. Hope everything's cool here. Call me if you need anything. I can't come round tomorrow—I'm tutoring a Year 7 kid—but I'll come over the next arvo and we'll get back to work on the DMO—The Dangerous Mystery of the Ormonds. OK?'

9:14 pm

I ate cheesy bread rolls for dinner, while thoughts of my great-uncle, and the blaze at 'Kilkenny' crept back into my mind.

As the birds rustled in the trees above, finding their roosts for the night, I studied the drawings by torchlight, trying to concentrate enough to make sense of them and the mysterious words of the Ormond Riddle.

Before long, I'd crawled into bed. Boges was right: the caravan was in a quiet spot, and once the sounds of the nearby traffic stopped and the surrounding suburb drifted off to sleep, I found it harder and harder to keep my eyes open.

I thought I heard someone calling my name and I struggled to sit up, but I couldn't move—my arms and legs felt like jelly.

I heard my name again.

'Yes?' I answered, my jaw almost refusing to move as I spoke, my voice no louder than a whisper.

It was Great-uncle Bartholomew. Standing by my bed.

'But you're dead,' I said. 'What are you doing here?'

He chuckled and tugged at his pilot jacket. 'It was a brilliant flight. Wasn't it? You flew it! The Ormond Orca soared like an angel!'

'But . . . but I crashed it,' I said. 'I'm so sorry. I didn't mean to. The Orca was destroyed. It was a bad landing. A really bad landing.'

Again came the familiar chuckle. 'Any landing you walk away from is a good landing, Cal.'

'But you . . . and "Kilkenny". It was all my fault.'

'Don't worry about me, or "Kilkenny",' he said, softly. 'The Ormond Orca flew, my boy! I always hoped it would, and I never knew whether I'd see the day. But because of you, I got to see it in action! It was incredible, wasn't it?'

'Uncle Bart,' I called after him, sensing that he was leaving. 'There are so many questions I want to ask you.'

His answer came from a great distance.

'You'll find the answers, Cal. That's a promise.'

I sat bolt upright and looked around. The caravan was empty and still, its dim shapes just visible in the moonlight that fell through the hole in the roof. There was no-one there but me. I had been dreaming again.

As I lay back down, I realised that the guilt and pain about Great-uncle Bartholomew that had been weighing on me was drifting away. Finally, I slept like a log.

7 JUNE

208 days to go . . .

4:41 pm

'I swear it was so real,' I told Boges as we sat on the bench in the caravan, sharing hot chips at the fold-out table. 'I could have sworn he was here—standing right there next to the bed, talking to me.'

'Maybe he was,' said Boges. 'Maybe he was speaking to you from another dimension. Some physicists reckon there's at least another twenty-two that we don't know about.'

'Don't tell me that. I have enough trouble surviving in just one dimension,' I said, pulling out the drawings and the Riddle and spreading them out in front of us.

'Dude, I have something for you,' he said, reaching into his backpack.

'A ticket home?' I asked, hit by a surge of homesickness. It had been so long since I'd lived in that ordinary, everyday life with my family. I'd been out on my own for almost six months now.

'I don't think so,' said Boges. 'This came yesterday. Registered mail.'

Frowning, I took a small package from him and opened it.

> Dear Cal,
>
> Here's the memory stick your father entrusted me with. I really hope it's helpful and meaningful for you in some small way.
>
> So happy to hear from you. Please keep in touch.
>
> Take care,
> Jennifer

'This is the memory stick I've been trying to get hold of,' I said, tipping the small gadget out of the padded envelope, and recalling the night I first met Jennifer at Labtech. The night that ended with escaped death adders.

'I know,' said Boges, with a grin. 'So you rang her then?'

'Yeah, just after you gave me her number. I rang Eric Blair again too, but . . .'

Boges saw the suspicious look on my face.

'What? Still off sick?'

I nodded.

'Something's not right there,' said Boges. 'Not right at all. We need to find him, soon. But for now let's deal with what we have here. The memory stick. I've already had a look at the files on my computer. I didn't think you'd mind.'

'Course not. What was on it?'

'They seem to be photos from Ireland,' he said. 'I'll show you.'

With that he reached into his school bag, pulled out his laptop, then plugged in the stick.

My excitement was building. Surely Dad's photos would be much more helpful than the drawings he'd done when he was sick. A photo is a photo, not some crazy drawing that we'd need to decipher to discover its meaning. I couldn't wait to see what I felt sure would be helpful clues, left by Dad before he contracted the UVI.

I waited expectantly as the first of the slideshow images filled the laptop screen.

'Wow!' I said, looking at the first few—pictures of a gloomy ruined castle with the moon rising behind it; the castle's empty, arched windows allowing strips of moonlight to fall on the stony floor; the crumbling towers sprouting young trees and weedy plants in silhouette. For a second, I was reminded of the Memorial Park cenotaph, when I first saw the moonlight shine through the stained glass window, illuminating the Ormond Angel. I hoped this was going to be as revealing.

'Where *is* that place?' I asked Boges.

He shrugged. 'Somewhere in Ireland, dude.'

'Oh really?' I said sarcastically.

'Hey dude, chill. There are lots of ruined forts and castles in Ireland. As soon as I saw these,' he said, indicating the pictures on the screen, 'I started chasing it on the net. I thought maybe it was a famous landmark—you know, like Camelot.'

'Camelot doesn't exist,' I reminded him. 'This place does.'

The ruined castle images were replaced by another picture, this time of a gate with the number '5' carved on it. It was in an elaborate Celtic design with long, scaly snakes and strange animals all weaving in and out of each other. Boges and I stared at each other, eyes wide.

'The "5" in Dad's drawings!' I said. 'Here it is in the photo!'

'Cool, huh?' said Boges. 'Looks like it could be

the address of some important place,' he said.

'And it's another number,' I said, thinking of Winter's words about a potential number riddle.

'It's a very particular and unique "5",' said Boges. 'One of a kind, my guess. Somewhere in Ireland.'

'Wow, Boges,' I said. 'You're really narrowing it down!'

'It'll all fall into place once we're in the right spot!'

The next image was a carved wardrobe or chest, almost as tall as a man, standing against a wall.

'These sure aren't tourist shots,' I said. 'I think they're very important and specific—but where are they and what do they mean?'

'Damn right they're important. Your dad went to great lengths to make sure you got them. I think he took them as part of his information-gathering about the DMO.'

'They must be things he saw that are somehow connected to the Ormond Singularity,' I interrupted. Suddenly everything seemed too hard. 'Fat lot of good they are to us, being in Ireland!'

'The ruin of an ancient castle,' said Boges, thinking aloud, 'the number "5" on a gate, and the wardrobe. I don't think we'll know what they mean exactly until we get there. And that could be a bit tricky.'

I knew he was feeling as disappointed as I was. I'd been hoping for a massive breakthrough—for some real clues from the time before Dad's mind became scrambled eggs.

I slammed my fist down on the table, and then jumped up in frustration.

Boges looked up at me and folded his arms. 'Cool it. These pictures don't make any sense right now, but when we get to Ireland—'

'When we get to Ireland? Are you kidding me? We're never going to get to Ireland! I can't even walk down the street without watching my back! How do you think I'm going to get to Ireland? And so what if we did? We walk around with a bunch of photos asking people, "Have you seen this? Or this?". It's just not going to happen!'

I started pacing up and down, angry and agitated. Everything was out of our reach. It was all impossible.

Boges didn't say anything, at first. He just turned away and looked at the laptop, flicking through the photos again.

'What are you doing?' I asked.

'What I can. Come on, Cal. I know this is messed up, but you can't lose it like that. We have to keep trying. These photos will mean something to us soon enough. But right now we need to focus on what we already know—*and* we need to keep trying to find out what the Ormond Singularity is.'

Boges pointed to where I'd been sitting. I stopped my pacing and stamping around.

'OK, OK,' I said. He was right. Raving on wasn't going to help us at all.

'Hey, what's that?' I said, noticing a new picture opening up.

'I just found it. It was in a different folder to the other pictures.'

As the photo opened and focused, I realised I was looking at a photo of a ruin, with my dad smiling in the foreground. I felt my chest tighten.

'It's your dad, dude.'

I couldn't speak. Boges turned to me. 'You OK?' he asked.

I nodded, but I didn't really feel OK. Seeing Dad's smiling face was . . . bittersweet.

'Can you zoom in?' I asked.

'Sure.'

Boges enlarged the photo, and Dad's face filled the screen. His eyes looked full of hope.

'You know what this means?' asked Boges.

'What?'

'It means your dad wasn't alone.'

He was right!

'But who was there with him?' said Boges.

'I don't know. The only person that I know was in Ireland with him was Eric Blair. If Eric took this photo, then maybe he knew about my dad's discovery. I wonder if Dad confided in him.'

'We've so got to find that guy already. Do you know where he lives?'

'No idea.'

'Leave it with me,' he said, scribbling a reminder in his notebook. 'I'll see what I can do. In the meantime, you have to tell me more about what happened in Mount Helicon.'

5:53 pm

We sat at the table and I told Boges about the solicitor's letter I found at Barney Helstrom's place and the receipt with the illegible signature, a record of who now held the documents concerning Piers Ormond's will. I made sure I told him about Skull and Crossbones, too, Helstrom's evil-looking dingo-cross killer dogs that almost ripped me apart.

'I just made it back to Bartholomew's place,' I said, 'when I found Oriana de la Force's car already waiting for me. That's when I ran inside and found him dying on the floor.'

Boges's eyes widened.

'He wasn't scared,' I said. 'It was like he was about to go on a real important solo mission. He talked about the chief pilot calling. I think he meant God or something.'

I wasn't sure about telling him the next bit, but I went ahead anyway.

'I've been feeling really bad about everything to do with him—blaming myself for his death, and the fire, and crashing the Ormond Orca. But after that dream the other night, after he spoke to me, I feel it's all OK. It was like him making peace with me. Or me making peace with myself. He was letting me know he was OK.'

Boges scratched at his wild mop of hair, and considered this for a moment before asking, 'So what happened after you found him on the floor?'

'I just sat there begging him to let me help him downstairs but he didn't want to go anywhere. All I could do was be with him. And then, I guess, he took off,' I said. 'Before he died, he gave me the name of the solicitor who has the Piers Ormond will.'

Boges's face lit up and his round face shone. 'Awesome! That's the next port of call. Why have you been withholding this important piece of information from your best buddy?'

'I haven't,' I said. 'I mean—I just didn't think of it until now—what with everything going on.'

'Cool, I get it. So what's the name?' he asked, flipping the elastic off his notebook again.

I opened my mouth to say the name that Bartholomew had told me—he'd made me repeat it to him as the fire started to race through the front of his house. But my mind drew a complete blank.

'The name, dude. *The name*. Give us the solicitor's name.' Boges had his pen poised, ready to write it down.

Again, my mind went back to how I'd crouched beside the dying body of my old great-uncle, the heat and smoke welling up the staircase, the sound of the blaze roaring downstairs, trying to get him to understand that he needed help, and him saying the name of the solicitor, making me repeat it. And I *had* repeated it. But somehow, it was gone from my memory.

I stared at Boges's expectant face.

'I can't remember,' I whispered, ashamed. The name just wasn't there. I had no idea—I couldn't even think of anything that might have been like the solicitor's name. I felt like there was something else that I was forgetting too. Something equally important. But all my mind could muster was fire and smoke.

'I can't remember,' I whispered again in disbelief. 'I can't remember it. He made me repeat it so that I wouldn't forget it.'

'But you have to . . .' said Boges. 'Just take a second to think about it.'

There was nothing I could say. I had totally failed.

'There was so much going on while I was trying to memorise it,' I said, lamely. 'It was like the end of the world in that place. But I'm sure that it'll come back to me. I've just gone blank for the moment.'

'I guess it's no use giving you a hard time over this,' Boges sighed. 'I wasn't expecting you to get early Alzheimer's disease, that's all.'

'After what I've been through in the last few months, it's a wonder I'm still going at all,' I snapped. 'You don't know what it's like. Always looking behind me. On the run day after day, night after night. Never knowing where the next meal is coming from, or if I've got a bed to sleep in. Maybe I am going nuts! Every night you sleep in your warm bed in your safe house after eating your mum's dinner. Do you know how many times I've almost been killed?'

Boges gave me a gentle punch in the arm, and smiled. 'You're right. That would have been the least of your worries when the fire started.

I was only joking around. Let's both forget about it for now and get stuck into something we *can* do.'

He opened up a website on his laptop.

'Look at this,' he said. 'I found it on this "Tudor gems" website.'

I leaned on the table next to him, and read:

THE ORMOND JEWEL

The Ormond Jewel, rumoured to contain an emerald the size of a pigeon's egg, and commissioned by Queen Elizabeth I, was one of a number of elaborate locket-style jewelled and enamelled rewards that the sovereign bestowed on her favourites.

The most famous of these rewards is the Drake Jewel, which Sir Francis Drake received after his victory over the Spanish. Most of these jewels, including the Ormond, the Suffolk and the Shrewsbury, are no longer in existence, having been broken up or sold at face value by impoverished nobility over the centuries.

Back to top | Next >>

'Broken up? Not true of the Ormond Jewel,' I said. 'I reckon Dad had it until it was stolen from our place.'

'We've gotta find it,' said Boges. 'Oh no, I've gotta run again. I still haven't done the Shakespeare assignment, and Mum thinks I'm at the library, which will be closed in a minute. I'll call in again soon. Maybe by then the name of the solicitor will have come to you.'

I lunged at Boges as he ran out of the van grinning.

13 JUNE

202 days to go . . .

Lot 2002 Jasper Road

6:46 pm

A week had passed and I hadn't remembered the name of the solicitor. It was gone. I figured that the stress I'd been under had wiped it from my memory. I gave up trying to extract it and hoped that it would just pop up one day when I was least expecting it. There was no reason for me to have faith in this technique—it never seemed to work at exam time.

Sometimes late at night or in the early hours of the morning, when the streets were mostly deserted and free from prowling cars, I left the caravan and went walking.

I was waiting for it to get late enough to go out, and started thinking back to the only death I'd had to deal with before we lost Dad—it was Gabbi's pet cat, Snuggles. She was the kind of cat Gab could dress up and sit in a stroller. She'd happily sit, purring, for hours, while Gab pushed her around the clothesline, and even out to say hello to the neighbours.

Snuggles had been missing for a day or two when I went out on my bike looking for her. I found her on some grass near the end of our street. She'd been hit by a car. I wrapped her in my jumper and carried her home.

Gabbi was so upset. There was nothing I could do to comfort her. She sobbed and sobbed until Mum came up with a great idea and suggested we organise a backyard funeral to say farewell to Snuggles. She took Gab's hand and they walked around the local park, picking pretty flowers, then came home and made a card together. Dad dug a hole behind the shed and as we buried Snuggles, Gabbi sang a song she'd just learned at school.

I thought about a lot of things Dad used to say—like that sometimes things happen that you don't like, but they lead to great things. I'd found that to be true. When I was a little kid, I really wanted to go to the school my neighbour was going to, but instead Mum enrolled me at Richmond Primary. I hated it at first, but if I hadn't gone there, I never would have met Boges.

Even so, I couldn't see myself ever looking

back on the UVI that killed my dad and thinking something great had come from it.

I needed to focus on the present, so as I walked outside, I put these things out of my mind and concentrated on trying to figure out who had the Ormond Jewel right now. Unless it had been taken by some third party we didn't know anything about, it had to be with Sligo or Oriana de la Force. More and more, I was convinced that it had been stolen from Dad's suitcase and that one of these criminal groups had it.

17 JUNE

198 days to go . . .

6:12 pm

The days and nights were getting colder. Sometimes I thought of Winter. A couple of times I went to call her but chickened out.

I had my phone in my hand again, ready to hit 'call'. But something stopped me.

6:23 pm

remembered the name yet? no pressure, lol.

nope!

didn't think so. i'm going to try and come round sometime tomorrow.

that would be awesome.

18 JUNE

197 days to go . . .

4:35 pm

I saw Boges unlocking the padlock on the gate and even before he could open his mouth, I said, 'No, I haven't remembered the name yet.'

He put his head down and walked through the long grass towards the caravan and me.

'I've been working with my uncle Sammy, cleaning rich people's houses,' he said as he stepped up into the caravan and dumped his school bag. He surprised me by slapping fifty dollars down on the table.

'Is that for me or are you just showing off?'

'That's for you. I've been raking it in; working with Sammy, selling more stuff on eBay, tutoring. Little Joseph Lee gets an "A" in maths, and I get rich. Do you know how much you owe me now?'

'I don't want to know,' I said. 'How about a share of the Ormond Jewel instead?'

'We gotta find it first.' Boges paused. 'Anyway,

I don't want to freak you out,' he said, 'but I've got to tell you something.'

'Spit it out,' I urged.

'I wasn't even sure if I should mention it . . . but on my way here, I saw Oriana de la Force sitting in her car talking to the guy who does the gardening at our school.'

An icy chill crept over me. She would never give up on finding me. Or finding the Riddle.

'At least she hasn't got me bugged any more,' I said. 'But she'll do whatever she can to hunt me down and get the Riddle back. And after the wild brumby trampling, I bet Sumo and Kelvin are bent on revenge more than ever.'

If I was Oriana de la Force, and suspected the person I was looking for was hiding out in the area, I'd be checking every possible place.

'Maybe I should think about moving again,' I said. As I was saying this, we both heard a car pulling up.

'Who's that?' said Boges.

I looked out the window. 'It's the sumo wrestler!' I shouted. 'He's here! He's parked on the other side of the road! We've gotta get out of here, quick!'

Boges instantly broke into a sweat, and feverishly grabbed his school bag, while I snatched up my backpack, stuffing everything in it. We couldn't run out onto the road, so instead we ran around the caravan and past the tree it was parked under. The paling fence of the adjoining property was no problem for me. My body had taken a battering, but I was becoming more and more agile. I was up and halfway over when I realised Boges needed my help.

'Grab my hand, Boges! Quick! You've gotta get over before we're spotted! Throw your bag first!'

He did as I said, and the bag hit me right in the face, nearly knocking me off the fence.

Finally, I was able to haul him over and we both fell on the other side.

'Hey, you two! What do you think you're doing in my backyard? I'll call the police!' threatened a woman who was waving a garden hose.

'Sorry, lady. But it's an emergency,' Boges puffed, getting himself up and grabbing his bag.

'We're leaving right now,' I added. 'Sorry!'

We bolted across her backyard while she continued yelling abuse at us, down the side of the house and down the front driveway into the next street.

Once there, I ducked instantly, pulling Boges down with me.

'Hide! Quick!' I hissed. We watched from behind some bushes as the dark blue Mercedes slowly cruised along the street.

Suddenly I heard the woman yelling again, along with heavy footsteps running down the side of the house! Sumo had followed us over the fence and was coming after us.

I grabbed Boges by the arm and dragged him out onto the street. Luckily, the Mercedes was about twenty metres away, executing a U-turn so that it could return to the house.

'This is our only chance!' I said. 'Let's make a break for it!'

We pounded up the road in the opposite direction to Oriana's car, running as fast as we could. We weaved and jumped fences, making our way up and across street after street until we were both exhausted. Eventually, we jumped on a bus that was on its way to the city. I didn't feel safe until we got off near the mall. But even then I wanted to make sure no-one was on our tail. Ducking and weaving past shoppers and around racks of hanging clothes, we ran right through the mall and out the other end, across the road, across the park and over to the clock tower. Maybe here we'd be safe. At least we could use the tower as a lookout position.

Clock tower

5:25 pm

I ran up the stairs two at a time and I could hear Boges grunting and puffing behind me. When we got to the top, there was a family group taking turns at looking through the telescope that pointed out to sea. They didn't take any notice of us as we collapsed against the high wall, sliding down, trying to get our breath.

'We can keep a lookout from here,' I panted, my heart thumping hard.

'What if they come up?' asked Boges, his face bright red and dripping with sweat. 'What do we do then? Jump?'

'They won't come up here,' I said, thinking quickly. 'It's too public. But now there's no way I can go back to the caravan. I'm going to have to find another place to live.'

Boges leaned over, his hands on his knees, puffing and panting. He shook his head.

'This is insane,' he said, between gulps of air. 'How do you keep doing it?'

'Simple. No choice,' I replied.

I watched my friend still trying to catch his breath. He wasn't cut out for this life. And I didn't want him in danger.

'Boges,' I said. 'I think you should maybe

back off a little. What if they recognise it's you helping me? They won't just *watch* your house in future . . . They'll . . . I don't want to think about what they could do. I don't want to put you and your family in more danger.'

My friend looked up at me, still breathless. 'I can't back off, Cal. If I back off, who will you have then? And anyway, if I'm not around, who will bug you about remembering the name of the solicitor?' he laughed. 'Come back yet?'

I slapped him on the back and pulled back a handful of sweat. 'Did you think that race we just ran might have jolted my memory? Don't worry, it's in here somewhere,' I said, tapping my forehead.

I stood up and looked over the parapet. A woman with bright, red hair caught my attention down in the park, and I quickly ducked down. But when I crept back up and looked more closely, I saw it wasn't Oriana de la Force, it was just another red-head, playing with some kids. I slunk back to the ground.

'Cheer up,' said Boges. 'We have another six months before the Ormond Singularity ends. Plenty of time.'

'Another six months . . . We've already had six months to find out about it and guess what? We hardly know anything.'

If the crazy guy from New Year's Eve was to be believed, then I had every reason to fear the end of the Ormond Singularity would kill me. But how could some ancient law kill anyone? He also said 'they' killed Dad, but Dad was sick, he wasn't murdered. Maybe the unknown virus had been attacking the crazy guy's brain too, making him say strange things, melting his synapses, just like what had happened to Dad. Whatever was going on, this constant countdown was sending *me* crazy.

Next month, I'd be turning sixteen and here I was, a wanted man, with the nation's law enforcement agencies all after me and worse than that, my own mum didn't believe in me. And now I had nowhere to live. The reality of my situation hit hard again. I was homeless. Where was I going to go tonight?

Boges slid down the wall and sat beside me.

'It'll be OK. I don't know how, but you've got me on the job, and everything's going to be OK. We have the Ormond Angel, we have the Ormond Riddle—or most of it—and now we're going to find a way to get the Ormond Jewel.'

'I'm thinking it's gotta be either Sligo or Oriana. But how can we know . . . ah, whatever.'

I sat up and scanned the people coming and going across the park, looking for Sumo or

Kelvin, or Oriana's red hair and dominant figure among them.

'I reckon Sligo has it,' said Boges after a pause.

'What makes you think that?' I demanded. 'Oriana hasn't let up on me. She's been coming after me forever! How do you know *she* doesn't have it?'

'I *don't* know that. Not for sure, anyway. She's coming after you now because she wants her Riddle back,' said Boges, in his logical, unflappable way. 'And it was like she was going after you before because she wanted more information, maybe about the last two lines. She never asked you about a jewel. Maybe she doesn't even know about it yet. You searched her place looking for the Riddle, and didn't come across anything about a jewel. I think the reason Sligo got hold of you that night at the car yard is because he already had the Ormond Jewel but knew that there was more he needed to know about the mystery of the Ormond Singularity than just the Jewel. I have a feeling he already has it safely stashed away.'

'A feeling? You don't normally go by "feelings". Aren't you all about facts?'

'What can I say, I'm changing,' he said with a smile.

'It's possible Sligo has it,' I said, nodding

slowly. I hadn't realised it until now, but Boges *was* changing. Not only was he thinking in new ways, he was tougher.

'Someone found out your dad bought the Jewel,' said Boges. 'And that someone broke into your place and knocked it off from his suitcase. I reckon that someone is Sligo. We need to break into his place.'

'And that would be easy, right? Just roll up there, stroll inside after kicking the door down, wander around searching the rooms until we find the Ormond Jewel. Piece of cake. And if Sligo stole the Jewel from Dad's suitcase in the first break-in, then who broke in later and attacked Gabbi and Rafe?'

'Dude, it could have been Sligo or Oriana. I just don't know. Either of them could have been there looking for more information. Gab and your uncle probably just got in the way. I still think Sligo's our best bet, so we need to find out.'

'We don't even know where he lives,' I said, before thinking of someone we both knew who could give us his address. I pulled out my mobile.

'Who are you calling?' Boges asked.

I waved his question aside before he could protest and waited until she answered. My face was flushing red, I was sure.

'Yes?'

Hearing her voice gave me a weird feeling in my stomach.

'It's Cal Ormond,' I said, trying to sound cool.

'Who?' she asked, and I imagined her frown angling her heavy eyebrows. 'Who am I speaking to?'

That flattened me. Was I that much of a distant memory already? Then I heard her giggle at the end of the line. I couldn't stop my mouth from smiling.

'Still wearing my skirt, "Cal Ormond"? Or did you buy a new one?'

'You've called Winter!' Boges's voice hissed in my ear. He shoved me. 'Look at that grin!'

'Shut up!' I said, covering the phone, and shoving him back.

'No more skirts for me, thanks. I need your help,' I admitted into the phone.

'You need me to bust you out of a psych ward again?'

'I need you to give me Sligo's address.'

'You wanna send him flowers?'

Boges's voice growled in my ear. 'What did she say?' he asked, leaning in to try and hear our conversation.

I pushed him away, got up and walked over to the other end of the now-empty tower.

'I think Sligo stole something of my dad's,' I said. 'And seeing as I helped you get something back from someone who had stolen from you, I was hoping you'd return the favour and help me do something similar.'

'You want to break into his place?' Winter's playful tone turned serious. 'Cal, that's way too dangerous. You'd never get past security without help. And I don't even know where he is right now,' she said. 'He moved out of the main house. Security reasons, he said. He didn't tell me where he was going, and I didn't ask.' There was a pause. 'Anyway, what did he take from your family? What is it that you're after?'

I hesitated. The old distrust swirled. I was aware of Boges pacing up and down on the other side of the tower.

'Let's get together,' I said, keeping my voice neutral, 'somewhere we can talk. I need your help to make a plan.'

'OK, I'll think about what's best to do. I'll call you when I'm free,' she said before hanging up.

'Well?' Boges asked.

'She doesn't know,' I said, putting my phone away.

'She doesn't know where Sligo lives?' said Boges, with a look of disbelief. 'I'm not so sure about that.'

'Why would she lie?'

'Because she can. Because she's Winter Frey.'

It seemed like Boges's admiration of Winter had been very short lived. He was right back to his old suspicions again.

'I know, I know, why the change of heart?' he said, like he'd read my mind. 'No real reason. I think she's cool. She *is* cool,' he corrected, 'but I just don't want us to mess up and let our guard down too much.'

There'd been no sign of our pursuers for a while, so we started making our way down from the tower.

'We've gotta find the Ormond Jewel. What else do you suggest?' I asked.

'I could try trailing Zombrovski,' Boges offered when I'd put my mobile away. 'I still catch him hanging round my place sometimes, hoping I'll lead him to you. I could try turning it round and hope he leads me to Sligo. But it's hard on the bike—keeping up with his car.'

'I don't know if that's a good idea,' I said, finding it hard to imagine Boges trailing such a big-time crim, tougher or not. I didn't want him putting himself on the line like that either, at least not without me around to try to back him up.

'I've gotta find another place to live,' I said.

It was getting late. And cold. 'Any suggestions?'

I'd come to the last few steps and leapt to the ground. I was so intent on looking out for the dark blue Mercedes on the street we had to cross to get to the park that I didn't see the guy who was barrelling down the footpath until he crashed into me. We both went down hard. I rolled and climbed to my feet, swearing.

'Hey! Watch where you're going!' I shouted.

'It's you!' he said as he got back to his feet. 'I was wondering when we'd run into each other again.'

'Griff?' I asked, ignoring the freckle-faced kid's bad joke.

Boges was looking at me expectantly, so I introduced them to each other, before leading us all down an alley. Griff's gelled hair was sticking up in tufts all over his head, and his eyes were wide open in surprise. He brushed a mark from his jeans and straightened his Nike jacket.

'There was someone I was trying to avoid,' he said, waving vaguely in the direction of the street. 'Wasn't looking ahead of me, sorry.'

'Who are you hiding from?' I asked, thinking he wasn't the only one with that problem. I couldn't take my eyes off his sneakers—they looked brand new and expensive. How could he afford them? They were the kind that gets their owners into serious trouble with gangs of rough kids who want to steal them.

'I can handle myself. Nothing serious,' Griff said, looking over his shoulder. 'I've lost them now.'

'So what have you been doing?' I asked, as the three of us started walking towards the beach. I had some half-baked idea that I might be able to find somewhere to sleep near the pavilion on the north end. 'What's it like living with your aunty?'

'Nah, that didn't work out,' said Griff. 'She didn't like my friends too much. I've been here and there, but right now I'm in a really nice place. I've got a room with a big TV and a balcony.'

'Really?' I asked, immediately interested.

'It's a private hotel—just back from the beach. Only eighty bucks a night. Special rates. I know someone,' he added, winking at me.

'Eighty bucks a night? Five hundred and sixty bucks a week?' scoffed Boges. 'Are you kidding?'

'How can you afford that?' I added.

'Easy! I've got a job. I made well over a grand last week.'

'A job doing what?' asked Boges, his eyes stuck on the gold Rolex Griff was wearing. It looked so bulky on his skinny little wrist. 'Robbing banks?'

Griff laughed. 'Your mate's a joker,' he said to me, while patting Boges on the back. 'No, not quite that kinda thing. I guess you could say I'm in the transport industry. Car recycling.'

Maybe car recycling was the way to go, I thought to myself as I remembered watching Winter sneak around Sligo's car yard. I'd suspected she was stealing car parts from there.

6:54 pm

We reached the beach and were heading up towards the pavilion, a large building that housed the Surf Lifesaving Association's clubhouse. Underneath this were change rooms with showers and toilets. Boges's mobile rang and he turned away to take the call. I could tell from the way he was speaking that his mum was on the line. Sure enough, he turned to us after hanging up and said, 'I've gotta go home in a minute. That was Mum. My uncle needs me to help out on a late-night cleaning job. One of his casuals called in sick. We need all the money we can get.'

'I've gotta go too,' said Griff, glancing at his watch. 'Actually, I gotta take off right now. But Tom if you want to work with me, you could make a lot of money. Why don't you call me and we'll talk about it?'

'OK,' I said, feeling a bit uneasy. Something about it didn't feel right.

Griff made sure I had his number, and then he hurried up the beach and disappeared.

'Boges,' I said, 'those jackets alone go for about three hundred bucks.'

'He's dodgy, *Tom*,' Boges said dubiously, using my fake name. 'Guys our age don't make a thousand bucks a week. Maybe he's just full of it.'

19 JUNE

196 days to go . . .

Bathers' Pavilion

12:02 pm

It was a rough, long, really cold night huddled in my sleeping-bag under the steps of the pavilion. I desperately needed a place to stay, somewhere safe, somewhere warm, where I could keep working on the information about the Ormond Singularity. Every day that went by brought midnight, December 31st closer. We needed to keep up the pace with putting all the pieces together.

I was eating some fish and chips out of a paper package when Boges rang.

'I found a guy who's willing to tell us where Sligo is,' he said, the second I picked up the phone. 'Or would you rather wait until your girlfriend finds out for you?'

'She's not my girlfriend!'

'Relax, I'm only joking. But this guy knows what he's talking about.'

'What guy? Who is he?'

'You won't believe it—I could hardly believe it myself—but last night I overheard Uncle Sammy, talking to this floor polisher guy in the building we were cleaning.'

'Yeah?' I said, anxious to hear what he had to say.

'So while I'm emptying office rubbish bins, and wiping down stair banisters, they're talking work—how it's been slow, the hours are tough, the money's poor—and then this guy, Jamie, starts talking about this massive job he's just started on. Polishing the floors at some "big crim's joint" . . .'

'No,' I said, wondering if I was misinterpreting Boges's hint. 'Not Sligo's new place?' I asked in utter disbelief.

'Got it in one! It's Sligo's new place! Can you believe it?! Dude, luck's so on our side right now!' Boges's voice boomed down the phone, excitedly. 'So this guy's banging on to my uncle about how massive the place is, and how they've just installed a safe in there that's the size of a broom closet!'

'I don't believe it!'

'Believe it! I nearly slipped down the stairs I was shining when I heard his name . . . and then about the safe! All I could see was the Ormond

Jewel! I got Jamie by himself later on, and tried to suss out where Sligo's place was. And that's when it got a little complicated.'

'C'mon, what happened then?!'

'He figured out pretty quickly how serious I was about getting the address, and he started talking money in exchange for information.'

'How much?'

'Information doesn't come cheap these days. He owes Sligo money for something. Something he'd rather forget, I'm guessing. He's paying him off with work on the house, but it turns out he's keen to pay the rest off in cash and get out of there.'

'How much?' I repeated.

'Four hundred.'

I pushed my fish and chips away with frustration. 'Where on earth are we going to get four hundred dollars?'

'Look,' said Boges. 'I can probably get a couple of hundred together in a week or so. But I'm not sure how long it will take me to get four.'

I brushed away the seagulls that were clustering around my fish and chips scraps. I hated this—always being dependent on Boges, living like a beggar.

'We don't have a chance then,' I said. 'Unless . . .'

Even though I couldn't see him, I could tell

Boges was already on the other end of the line shaking his head.

'Unless,' I continued, 'I call Griff.'

'Wait up, I don't know if that's such a good idea. He could be more trouble than he's worth,' Boges warned. 'Where does someone like him earn money like that? It can't be legit.'

'Boges, I don't really care. I can't pick and choose where I get cash from these days. We have to find out where Sligo lives. We've gotta find out whether he has the Ormond Jewel. Everything else is useless without it.'

'We'll figure something out. So where'd you sleep last night?' Boges asked, changing the subject.

'Beneath the pavilion stairs. And I nearly froze to death, no joke.'

'Well tonight won't be like that,' he said. 'Meet me around five at the clock tower.'

'What do you mean?' I asked.

'Be patient, my man. I might have some more good news for you.'

Clock tower

4:50 pm

'Hey!' said Boges, approaching me where I waited, his grin growing wider the closer he got to me.

He was swinging a key around on his finger. 'Something awesome awaits you, buddy. Let's go. Follow me.'

'What is it?'

'Just wait and see.'

5:28 pm

The sun was setting and pink clouds stained the sea a pale purple. A few seagulls swooped around us then lifted back into the air.

'You're going to love this,' he said, 'but you've got to be invisible.'

I looked at him, mystified.

'It will all become clear any moment now.'

At this point, we'd crossed Enid Parade, and I hurried behind Boges as he made his way towards a group of houses on the headland. I couldn't understand why we were walking towards a white and blue mansion that stood in tropical gardens overlooking the sea. We reached the gates and Boges paused in front of them.

5 Enid Parade, Crystal Beach

5:59 pm

'We're not about to spring into Sligo's place, are we?' I asked.

'No way! My uncle cleans this house, and I

pinched the spare key,' he said, opening the gate and showing me the way through tropical vines growing on trellises over the garden.

'The owners are away,' Boges continued, 'so I thought—'

'You thought I could stay here while they're gone? In a mansion?'

Boges beamed. 'What do you think?'

I looked around. Because of the rise of the land and the way the mansions were set back from the road, it was completely secluded and private. It was a cool idea, but I wondered if it was really possible I could get away with it.

Boges led me up the stairs alongside the driveway that led to the front doors. As I got closer, I could see it was an absolutely amazing place—three levels, glassed-in balconies, all overlooking the landscaped terraces and across to the sea.

'Boges,' I said, as he opened the front door, and I stepped up behind him, 'are you sure about this?'

'Completely. They're overseas for six months. It'll be cool as.'

'But what about *them*?' I asked, instinctively pulling my hoodie half across my face as I pointed to the security cameras near the entrance.

'I've already taken care of it. I worked on the system: put it on a loop so that the logging tape repeats the same twenty-four hours of fugitive-free footage. I've done the same for the cameras inside. In a few days I'll alter the lighting and shake it up a bit to make it even more convincing,' he said, excitedly. 'Come on, it's cool.'

'When did you have time to do that?'

'Cal, that stuff doesn't take me long.'

6:03 pm

I followed Boges inside, as we both pushed the heavy doors open. It was awesome. We stood staring at an incredible foyer, with this huge, fancy staircase curling up to the next two levels. Ahead was a wall of glass, framing a breathtaking landscape view of the ocean rolling in long waves onto the beach. I stood for a moment, taking it all in. I'd never seen anything like it before. It was so different from the world I'd been living in this year.

'You know how the scientists say we should be living in a way that leaves only a light carbon footprint?' asked Boges. 'You have to live in this place without leaving any footprint at all. Well, that's not entirely true; you can use everything, but really discreetly. The owners will expect my uncle to be using a small, but fairly constant flow of electricity to do the cleaning and maintenance. So a little won't hurt.'

He took my backpack from me and propped it up against the wall. Boges took out his old Polaroid camera and started noisily snapping photos of the living room area.

'You sleep in here on the floor in your sleeping-bag,' he said, 'and you don't leave a trace of yourself. Try to stick to this level. It's the perfect spot because you are completely hidden from any of the neighbours. No-one will see you if you stay here.'

'I don't think I'll be coming and going anywhere for a while,' I said, looking around at all the comfort and luxury.

Boges pressed a button in the wall, and heavy curtains moved across the huge windows and glass doors, completely covering them, so that the interior became very dim, like night had fallen in seconds.

'Try not to use any lights at night,' ordered Boges, 'unless the curtains are completely closed. Maybe you could use candles. On second thoughts, don't. I don't want you setting fire to the place. Avoid using anything in the fridge—not that there is much. Anything you move or use put it back—in exactly the same place. OK?

That's why I've taken these photographs,' he said, spreading a bunch of still-developing Polaroid pictures across the kitchen bench. 'So you can compare how things look.'

I took a few more steps around the place, walking down the hall, finding more spacious and luxurious rooms.

'This is fantastic,' I said when I returned. 'Imagine living in this place for real!'

'Crazy, right?' Boges dug into his bag. 'Here, you can use this if you need it. Runs on batteries.' He passed me a small plastic thing that looked like a candle, but wasn't. 'Flick the switch on the bottom.'

I did as he said, and the little light flickered on with a candle-like glow.

With the touch of a switch, a gas heater fired up on low, and warmed the room. We sprawled on the thick, white carpet. I would have to be very careful with that, I thought.

6:30 pm

'Let me know if you have any ideas on how to get that money together,' said Boges as he was leaving.

'You too. And let me know if I have to get out of here fast for any reason.'

'Cool. I'll call you again soon. Lastly–' Boges

stopped in the doorway to pull something else out of his bag. It was a towel. 'Clean yourself up, will ya?'

20 JUNE

195 days to go . . .

9:25 am

In the morning I filled up the bathtub and had the best soak of my life. I hacked at my hair a bit, and afterwards made sure I left no trace of it in the sink. When I looked at myself in the mirror, I smiled. I felt strangely good. The bruises on my face from the Orca crash had faded almost entirely, and while I could still see that I was me, I didn't think I looked much like the Cal who ran away from home months ago. I made coffee from some supplies Boges had left me, and toasted some bread.

I stared at the sea for a while and although this house was incredible, I wished for the warmth and familiarity of my old home back in Richmond, with Gabbi and Mum. If I ever wanted that dream to come true, I had a lot of work to do. I knew what my next step had to be. Calling Griff Kirby.

10:31 am

'I was wondering whether I'd hear from you,' he said.

'I need money,' I said. 'I've got to earn four hundred dollars–fast. So what can I help you with?'

'You're talking to the right person,' said Griff. 'I always knew we would be a good team. From the moment I tried to knock off your backpack in the bush and you tackled me down.'

I couldn't help smiling. Griff was likeable even though it was obvious he was a scammer from way back.

'I can guarantee you *five* hundred dollars. No sweat. I usually work with three other guys. Meet me at the Liberty Mall carpark at a quarter to seven tonight. Level C, blue.'

'But everything will be closed by then,' I said. 'What's the job?'

'Just be there. OK?'

Carpark
Liberty Mall
6:45 pm

It was dark as I rushed towards the familiar carpark. I was feeling uneasier with every step, but I tried to leave my doubts behind me and focus on the five hundred dollars that would pay for the information I needed.

I slipped past the boom gates and up the fire stairs. There were hardly any cars left on the upper levels now, as most people had left for the day. As I approached Level C I could hear dull voices and Griff's laugh nearby. I followed the sound around a corner and towards the ramp. Apart from the small group of guys standing in the furthest corner, there was only one car there, a red BMW sports car, parked in one of the reserved spaces. Griff turned around as I neared.

'Tom! Good to see you. The gang's all here. We haven't got much time,' he glanced at his Rolex. 'She should be here in about eight minutes.'

She? I wondered.

Griff introduced me to the three other guys he was standing with.

'Everyone, this is my mate Tom. Tom, meet the guys. This is Freddy.' I nodded to a lean, sallow guy with a shaved head and tight jeans. 'Dogs.' I nodded to Dogs, a solid guy with an army-style camouflage jacket. Griff raised his voice, 'And lastly this is Three-O.'

Three-O put out his hand out to shake mine. His hold felt like it would break my fingers. As I pulled away I saw that he only had three fingers on his right hand. He had slicked-back hair, a scar across his eyebrow and his lips were in a sneer. I knew these guys already—they were the jerks in the stormwater drain that chased me and almost got me killed in the floodwater. Luckily they didn't seem to recognise me.

Three-O turned to Griff. 'You sure this guy's cool?'

'He's cool,' Griff reassured.

'So what's the job?' I asked.

Three-O pointed to the BMW. 'That is,' he said.

'I don't get it,' I said, looking to Griff for an explanation, but all he did was shrug his shoulders, wearing a silly grin on his face.

'You said he was cool.' Three-O snarled at Griff. 'Who is this guy?'

'He's cool, he's cool,' Griff repeated, glancing at me. 'He just didn't know exactly what the job was today.'

'He reckons he doesn't *get it*,' Three-O laughed wickedly. 'But he will. You'll get it,' he said, staring at me.

Freddy and Dogs laughed—and it wasn't a good sound now, just as it hadn't been the first time I'd heard it, echoing through the drains.

'OK, we're almost out of time,' said Three-O. 'Get into position.'

Griff's three companions disappeared behind one of the wide, supporting carpark pillars.

'What's going on?' I asked, as Griff pulled me behind another pillar.

'Simple redistribution of wealth,' he said. 'We only take from people who can afford it.'

I looked across at the red BMW. 'Redistribution of wealth?' I said. 'You mean you're going to steal this car?' I asked. 'That's a crazy idea. You won't be able to. They're all microchipped these days.'

'We're going to steal this car. We wait till it's unlocked,' Griff explained, 'then we take it. It's easy. They claim the loss through their insurance. They don't lose anything but the time it takes to make a couple of phone calls. They just buy another car. It's not really a crime because nobody gets hurt and nobody loses.'

What Griff was saying made a strange kind of sense. But was it really a victimless crime? I was desperate to get that money. Maybe desperate enough to convince myself no-one was getting hurt.

'What happens next? After you've got the car?' I asked.

'We take the car to a guy called Kenny Salvo. He makes a few adjustments to it, different colour, new engine number, and bingo! A new car! Tom, I can guarantee you five hundred lazy dollars—just for helping. Easy money. *No-one* gets hurt.'

Griff suddenly pulled me back behind the pillar as a woman wearing a cream suit, clipped down the ramp in her high-heeled shoes, heading towards the red BMW. Her confident walk and her outfit reminded me a bit of how Mum used to be. She shifted her handbag around and pulled her car keys out.

That's when I realised she was going to be the victim of this *victimless* crime! I watched while she unlocked the car and slid into the driver's seat. A few moments later, the engine and the headlights came on. I felt frozen, with a sick feeling welling up in my stomach, unable to stop what I knew was going to happen next.

Griff and the boys jumped out from their hiding places and exploded into action. Within seconds, Freddy, Dogs and Griff had surrounded the BMW, while Three-O wrenched the driver's door open and barked, 'Get out, now!'

The woman's face distorted with fear, and tears streaked make-up down her face. Everything in me knew this was wrong, wrong, wrong.

'Come on!' Dogs barked at me to join them at the car.

'What are you doing? Stop this!' cried the woman, as she struggled to get out while avoiding Three-O's menacing bulk. 'Please! Let me go!'

Stunned, I watched while Griff leaned into the car past the woman and pulled the keys from the ignition.

'Give those to me!' Three-O yelled. 'I'll drive!'

I couldn't stand by and let this happen. I had to do something.

'Stop!' I yelled, finally running over to the group around the car, wrenching them away from her. 'Leave her alone! Get away from her!' I threw myself on Three-O who had his back to me as he pushed the woman away from her car.

She stepped back, unwittingly towards Dogs and Freddy, who grabbed her, one on each side, as she fell on her knees. Somehow she twisted an arm free and dived for her mobile. Dogs kicked it from her hand and it skidded along the oil-stained cement floor of the carpark, metres away from her.

'You have no right to take my car!' she gasped, struggling between the two guys. 'Let me go! Let me go!'

Three-O twisted around to face me, and wrenched my hands from his shoulders.

'What do you think you're doing?' he snarled, grabbing me round the throat.

'Griff!' I croaked, trying to pull Three-O's hands away from my neck. 'You said no-one would get hurt! But look what's happening! One woman! And you're attacking her four to one!'

I thought of the recent break-in at Rafe's place, and how my mum had been terrorised and injured by an unknown assailant's cowardly assault. I grabbed at Three-O's hands around my throat and tore them off me.

'Griff, give me the damn keys!' hissed Three-O, releasing one hand to lunge for them.

Griff hesitated, looking from me to Three-O.

'I thought you were a decent guy, Griff,' I panted. 'Not a coward. Let her go!' I shouted to Freddy and Dogs, so angry that I'd forgotten just how outnumbered I was. 'Let her go!'

'Here's the knight in shining armour,' sneered Three-O, lunging at me again. I jumped out of his reach. He was torn between grabbing the keys from Griff and getting away with the car, or dealing with me. 'The carpark hero,' he jeered. 'Let me put you in the picture, hero boy. I give the orders round here. Now rack off!' he rushed at me, but I dodged him again.

'Griff,' I called, hoping I could convince him, 'don't give him the keys!'

'Look out!' the woman screamed.

But her warning came too late.

I didn't realise Three-O was behind me until the first punch landed. I was shocked, winded, and before I could even turn around, a second punch landed in my side. I stumbled against a cement pillar.

'Get off him!' shouted Griff's voice. 'Here, take the keys! Take them!'

Painfully, I twisted to throw Griff a grateful glance when a harder punch sent me sprawling.

'We've gotta get out of here!' I heard one of the guys yell. A high-pitched sensation in my ears turned out to be the carpark alarm.

'You fool!' I heard Three-O screech at Griff. 'You've ruined everything. Why did you bring this loser along? I'm not working with you any more. Never again!'

Fast footsteps faded as they bolted away.

A few moments later, I felt myself being helped to my feet. I opened my eyes, blinking to clear my head, and found the concerned face of the woman who'd been attacked very close to mine. She had freckles under her make-up and clear, green eyes.

'Thanks,' I muttered. 'I'm so sorry for what they did to you. We've gotta get out of here.'

'No need,' she said. 'They've gone. Little

cowards ran like rats once the alarm started. I'm so sorry for what they did to you. At least the smaller one had the decency to give me my keys back.'

I looked past her to see Griff Kirby standing at the top of the ramp near the exit. His eyes met mine, and then he too vanished.

My ribs were killing. I leaned against the pillar, trying to regain my strength and my balance, wondering how I would ever move again. I realised how lucky I was not to have been too badly injured. I started moving my arms and legs. Everything still seemed to work.

'Are *you* OK?' I asked the woman. I could see she wasn't. Her stockings were ripped at the knees, which were bloody from when she'd fallen. Her whole body was trembling with shock but there was a fighting light in her eyes.

She nodded. 'I'm fine. Just sorta . . . shaken up.'

She took a step back and leaned against the red car, briefly closing her eyes, catching her breath. After a few moments, she shook her head as if to clear it and took a deep breath.

'We should get you to the hospital,' she said, before extending her hand to me. 'My name's Belinda Quick.'

'Cal,' I said, taking her hand, then stopped short, realising I'd let my name slip.

'How can I ever thank you? You need help. Let me drive you to a hospital. I think a doctor should check you out. That guy really gave you a beating. What a brute, hitting you from behind!'

I shook my head, my back aching with the movement. 'No,' I muttered, 'no doctors. I'll be fine.'

She scanned the floor for a moment, before cautiously stepping over to pick up her phone from where it lay. She started dialling.

'No! What are you doing?'

'Calling the police.'

'Please,' I begged her. 'Don't!'

'I have to! They just assaulted me, and tried to steal my car. And look what that guy did to you!'

'Please,' I begged again. 'I shouldn't have been with them. I don't want to get into any more trouble. My parents will kill me if they find out I was with those guys again,' I lied.

Belinda gave me a slow and steady, knowing look.

'Can I give you a lift then?' she offered. 'You need to get home. I'll drop you off before I go to the police station.'

I knew I couldn't walk very far just then, so

I had to hope she was being honest and wouldn't drag me straight to the police. With Belinda's help, I got into her BMW and asked her to drop me off near the beach.

'My dad works in the pavilion,' I lied again.

'And he'll be there at this hour?'

'Yes,' I said. More lying. 'Thanks, Belinda.'

'Thank you,' she said. 'I don't know what would have happened if you hadn't helped me.'

She passed me a business card from her wallet when we pulled up along the path to the pavilion. 'Promise me you'll stay away from those kids?'

'Promise.'

I waved as I watched her drive away in her red BMW, then I limped over to a chair and collapsed on it. I felt exhausted and drained of all energy. Everything ached. I needed to pull enough strength together to get myself back to Enid Parade.

5 Enid Parade, Crystal Beach

9:00 pm

I found some painkillers in the bathroom cupboard and I hoped no-one would notice two of them missing. I washed my face and changed my clothes before rolling out my sleeping-bag and lying down, listening to the waves. What was I going to do now? I didn't have my five hundred dollars, I didn't know where Vulkan Sligo lived, and I looked like a punching bag again.

I kept reliving the horrible scene in the carpark. The choice I'd made had pretty much made itself. I'd instinctively jumped forward to help that woman. I tried imagining things differently, if I hadn't done that. That I'd shut up and helped them with the car-jacking and went home with five hundred dollars in my wallet. But I imagined Belinda Quick, frightened and bleeding, left alone in the carpark without her car, shocked and possibly injured. How could I have lived with myself if I'd gone down that road? And it wasn't true that I'd only got a big fat zero from the whole incident. I was slowly realising that I'd kept something very important to me—my own basic goodness. My own self-respect.

21 JUNE

194 days to go . . .

9:34 am

I dragged myself back to the bathroom and checked myself again in the mirror. I checked out my ribs where Three-O had punched me. Luckily, my body didn't look as bad as I thought it would last night. Apart from a graze on my cheekbone from where I'd hit the ground, I could hide my injuries under my clothes.

As the hours ticked by, I couldn't stop picturing the Ormond Jewel lying in a safe at an address I didn't know, guarded by Vulkan Sligo and his henchmen. It haunted me. I was determined to find out whether he really had it . . . and take it back from him. But how?

I smoothed my hair down and put on a pair of glasses Boges had given me the other day. With their heavy black frames against my pale skin, they gave me a nerdy look.

Today I wanted to go to the city. I wanted to

take a closer look at the cenotaph. On the way out the front door, I felt something in my pocket. I pulled it out.

BELINDA QUICK
ATTORNEY AT LAW

Suite 10, 2/501 Florence St
Liberty Square, 51032
[P] +052 8976 1200 [E] b.quick@law.net

I wondered if she knew Oriana.

11:42 am

Sunshine blazed through the stained glass at the cenotaph, causing the Ormond Angel to glow with coloured light. I walked around to get the best angle. I wanted to get a closer look at whatever decoration the Angel was wearing near his gas mask.

There was no doubt something was there. It looked like a green stone set in gold. We thought before that it was a medal. Could this have been the Ormond Jewel?

I sat down in the darkest corner, silently staring up at the Angel.

12:55 pm

Someone called my name, and I spun around, knowing the familiar voice in seconds.

'Cal,' she said. 'I'm always hoping I'll run into you here.'

Today Winter's wild hair was pulled back from her face and tied with a black ribbon. She was wearing a loose white top, a black, woollen scarf, and tight black jeans with her white sneakers. She looked different. Good, different.

'What are you doing here?' I asked, quickly whipping off the nerdy glasses.

'I didn't know you wore glasses. Oh, your face,' she said, almost touching my grazed cheek with her hand.

'Someone put me on the ground last night,' I said.

'You want to talk about it?'

'Another time,' I said.

'So what are you doing here?' she countered.

'You first,' I said.

'No. I insist.'

'OK,' I said, after a pause. 'I'm here to look again at what the Angel is wearing on his chest—not the gas mask—that other thing.'

She took a few steps closer to the stained glass window, staring at the Angel with her dark eyes. 'It's some sort of medal. Maybe a war medal? Green and gold.'

Her intense eyes turned in my direction. 'Do you know what it is?'

'I do,' I said. 'I think it's the Ormond Jewel.'

'What is it with this Ormond family? Ormond Angel, Ormond Riddle, and now this Ormond Jewel. Do you Ormonds have to attach your name to everything?'

'Sounds like it,' I said, a bit embarrassed. I looked around, feeling unsafe even saying these words aloud. 'It's something that used to be in our family. It's part of the double-key code.'

'The double-key code! Is it part of the mystery?' she asked eagerly. 'Like your dad's drawings?'

'Winter,' I said, avoiding her question for now. 'I've told you why I'm here, now it's your turn.'

'But you already know why I come here. I come here all the time. I come here when I need to think.'

'What about?' I asked.

'Lots of things. I sometimes think of you,' she said to the ground. 'I heard about what happened in the carpark with Griff Kirby last night—that was you with him, wasn't it?'

'You know Griff? What–you know what happened?'

Winter smiled. 'Thought so,' she said, as she played with her hair, twisting the black ribbon in her fingers. 'I saw the graze on your face and thought straight away that you must have been "the new kid" they were talking about. I know almost everything that happens around here.'

'But they don't know it was me, do they?'

'Don't think so. I didn't hear your name.'

We were almost at the park gates before I realised we were walking away from the cenotaph.

'So what else have you been thinking about?' I asked her. 'Giving me Sligo's new address?'

She stopped walking and turned to me. For a moment I thought she was going to say something, but then her dark-brown eyes flickered away and she said nothing.

'Winter, I need to find out where Sligo is. Because wherever he is, that's where the Ormond Jewel is,' I said. 'I think,' I added.

'Come back to my place and we can talk,' she offered. 'We'll be safer there.'

'Your place? I don't think so.'

'I don't live with Sligo! I told you, I don't even know where he is right now!'

'How can you not know where he is? I think–'

'Don't think. Just walk,' she ordered. With that, she took my hand and pulled me along with her.

12 Lesley Street

2:10 pm

We stopped at an old, run-down apartment building.

'So this is where you live?' I asked.

'I live—*on my own*,' she stressed, 'around the back and up the top.'

She led me down the side of the building, past a narrow garden and some empty car spaces, around to the back, where several lines of washing and a row of garbage bins took up most of the yard.

'Up there,' she said, pointing to a flight of stairs that ran up the outside of the building like a fire-escape. 'My place is up the top. Can you hear the wind chimes? They're outside my window.'

We clanged up the staircase, the delicate clinking of the chimes becoming louder as we came to the flat roof of the building and stepped onto it. It was a big area about the size of a tennis court, with a one-and-a-half metre high brick wall around the edge, lined with long timber flowerpots, in which grew rich red, pink and white geraniums like Mum had planted back at our place in Richmond. In the middle of the rooftop stood a small building, not much larger than a double garage. Above one of the two front windows were the wind chimes Winter mentioned. They were made of long pieces of purple glass that hung together like teardrops.

'It's a caretaker's flat,' Winter explained, unlocking the front door. 'It's only tiny,' she said, 'but it suits me. Sligo owns most of the building and that means I get to live here without paying rent.'

I followed her into her tiny home, looking around in wonder. The place reminded me of Winter herself. The windows were draped with the same sorts of filmy shawls and scarves that she wore, in mauves and blues, casting soft, coloured sunlight into the room. The bed in the corner was covered with silky purple and white fabric, and had this iron bedhead with posts that curled into spiral shapes. In the other corner were a sink and bench, with a microwave oven and a cooktop, and a small table with two mismatched wooden chairs.

'Cool,' I said, looking around. 'I love the walls,' I said, noticing a swirling shape of tiny birds drawn up the wall beside her bed.

'I did those,' she said. 'Just in black ink. I

have a bit of a thing for birds. And for drawing them. Always have. I'll make us some tea?'

She switched on the electric kettle and busied herself in the tiny kitchen area while I kept looking around. A black-and-white photo of her parents sat alone on a clean, white desk under one of the windows. I recognised the couple, recalling seeing them in Winter's heart-shaped locket a while ago. Her mum's fair, sweeping, slightly wild hair fell on her shoulders, beside her dad, who had classic Chinese features, and radiated strength and determination. I looked across at Winter where she was opening a new packet of tea bags, thinking again that she looked a little like both of them.

All around the mirror on the dressing table she'd attached tiny birds, cleverly made with real feathers, felt, beads and fabric. Sparrows, colourful finches like Boges used to have when he was younger, and a little blue bird that, along with the ink art on the wall, reminded me of the tattoo on her wrist. A birthday card with a picture of a cupcake was tied with thin ribbon to a hook on the mirror.

'It was my birthday last week,' said Winter, looking over her shoulder at me as she grabbed down two mugs from the cupboard above the sink. 'Sixteen now. How old are you?'

'Happy birthday,' I said, sitting down at the little table. 'I'll be sixteen at the end of next month,' I said, 'but I won't be getting any birthday cards.'

'You might,' she said, turning to me with a half smile.

I smiled back.

'How come you have your own place?' I asked. 'I don't know anyone my age that lives on their own.'

Winter stirred milk into the mugs. 'You should talk! You're *fifteen* and living on your own.'

'That's different,' I argued. 'That wasn't my choice.'

'I know,' said Winter. 'I just kept nagging Sligo, saying that I couldn't study at his place, that I needed a quiet spot for my schoolwork. He's crazy about education. Mine, anyway. He thinks a "young woman like me" should be well-educated. So he gave in, and offered this place to me. It's cool,' she said, 'not having to answer to anybody, and being able to do what I want when I want . . . but it does get a little too quiet sometimes. Anyway, Sligo does check in on me every now and then.'

'Really?' I asked, suddenly nervous.

'Don't worry, he always calls me first. So what date in July is your birthday?'

The thought of my birthday brought with it the sad memory of my dad's death.

'What's wrong? You look really sad, Cal. Don't want to grow up?'

'It's not that,' I said. 'My dad died the week before my birthday. I was thinking of that. He's been gone for almost a year.'

Winter looked surprised at what I'd said. She stopped what she was doing and put both her hands on her hips.

'My parents died *on* my birthday,' she said, lowering herself into the chair beside me.

Her face had dropped, and she looked defeated. I wanted to put my arms around her.

'That sucks,' I said, as usual not knowing what to say. 'So you've just had the anniversary of their deaths?'

She nodded.

'Do you want to talk about it?' I asked.

She shook her head and reached back for our mugs. 'Not right now. But some other time, OK,' she said, passing me mine.

I hoped she would open up to me one day. I wanted her to trust me. And I was curious about what happened to her parents, and how she'd ended up in Sligo's care.

The cupcake birthday card in my line of sight kept grabbing my attention. I wondered who it was from. I found myself trying to read what was written inside. When I looked away, I noticed a diary with its pages open on Winter's bed. It was impossible not to read the question that was written on one page in bold letters: 'How much of myself have I given away, to get the things I want?'

I quickly turned my eyes away from the diary, but the question Winter had written there kept repeating in my head. How much of myself was I giving away in my quest to discover the truth about the Ormond Singularity? How much of himself had my dad given away? His life?

I felt strangely peaceful and happy sitting in Winter's cosy flat—things I hadn't felt for a long time. Just for that moment, we were an average guy and girl sharing a drink. Except we weren't average—one of us was the adopted daughter of a major criminal and the other was me, a teen fugitive.

'OK, tell me the whole story, please,' Winter said, getting up and pulling a curtain aside to peer down onto the grounds of the building. 'The Ormond Jewel?'

I looked at her face when she turned back to me. She didn't say anything more, just sat down calmly sipping her tea again. Finally, she leaned closer to me. 'You still don't trust me, do you?'

'I'm trying to,' I said. I suddenly felt uncomfortable. There was an awkwardness that I didn't have time to think about too much because she started speaking again.

'We're alike, Cal,' she said. 'We're both stuck in situations we don't want to be in. We both end up doing things we don't want to do. We understand each other.'

'But you've got your own place,' I said, looking around the little flat, wanting to change the subject. 'You're not in the situation I'm in—an outlaw with a price on my head.'

'No,' she agreed, 'not in the way you are. This place is rent-free, yes, but I do pay a price for living here.' she said. 'I have no parents—I'm alone, like you. I don't live an ordinary life like other girls my age. No family life—I don't go to school. I'm a sort of fugitive too.'

'A fugitive from who?' I asked, frowning.

She started twirling a strand of her hair around her fingers. 'I don't like the answer to that,' she said, 'so I won't say.' She paused. 'Vulkan is using me, I know that much. It's hard to believe, but he desperately wants to be—well—respected.'

'You said that once before, but I don't get it.'

'He's obsessed. He wants to shed his criminal image. He wants to wipe his past—of poverty and crime—from everyone's memories, especially his own. His most recent effort was donating money to the city ballet company—he wants to be the patron of the ballet, can you believe it? He wants to be seen as a respectable, honourable member of society. And that's where I come in.'

I remembered the previous conversation we'd had about this—her family being wealthy people. But this time, it didn't sound so incredible. I'd lived long enough as an outcast to understand wanting another life.

'I feel like he's taken me under his wing just so at some point he can parade me around like some royal princess, while making sure everyone knows that I was once a poor, little orphan girl he single-handedly saved from a life on the streets.'

'But you came from wealth didn't you?'

'Yeah, but there was nothing left when Mum and Dad were killed.'

'Killed?'

'By the accident,' she explained, quickly. 'It's like he thinks he can earn respect by showing people what he's done for me. I think it's all for show. Not because he actually wants me to have those things . . . Oh, I don't know.'

'I think I know what you mean,' I said, watching her go to the window again. 'What's so interesting downstairs?'

'Nothing,' she said, but my question seemed to have rattled her. 'I saw you looking at my diary before,' she said, returning to the table and sitting down again.

'I didn't mean to snoop,' I said. 'The page was open. I just saw that one line.'

'Don't worry,' she continued. 'I don't mind.'

'Reading that makes me think of all the things I've given away. Like my real self—for starters.' I tapped the nerdy glasses that I'd put on the table.

'But you've had to,' she said, 'to prove your innocence. To survive. You haven't had a choice.'

She stood up and took our mugs to the sink, slowing near the window again.

'I know I'm difficult and sometimes I'm unreliable,' she said, not looking at me. 'I'm always kinda distracted. I have my own . . . discoveries to make. I said before that I was a fugitive from something . . . I feel like I'm a fugitive from myself and my memories. The accident that happened on my birthday . . . it wouldn't have happened if I hadn't—'

'You can't blame yourself for an accident,' I said, filling the silence. I could see that was the end of it. She wasn't going to tell me any more.

'I do want to help you, Cal. But to do that, I need to know the whole story. Not just the scraps I've picked up along the way. I want to know everything behind this Ormond mess. The *DMO*—is that what you and Boges call it?'

'That's right. The DMO.'

It was so quiet and peaceful up in Winter's rooftop place. And even though she was acting a little restless, danger seemed far away and impossible. Right now she was sitting close to me, giving me her full attention. And so I began. I told her everything.

Everything. I told her about Dad dying after his trip to Ireland, and the earliest incident with the crazy man late last year, who told me to keep away from the Ormond Singularity if I wanted to live through the next three hundred and sixty-five days. I told her everything bad that had happened since then, and all the clues I'd uncovered so far about the drawings, the Ormond Angel, the Riddle, the Jewel and the Singularity. And about the people who'd helped me along the way. Winter listened carefully, occasionally nodding her head.

'Since meeting my great-uncle,' I said, 'I've discovered that without the Ormond Jewel, the Riddle and the drawings are useless.'

'And these clues are supposed to lead to the Ormond Singularity?' she asked, leaning closer.

'That's the theory,' I said. 'The Ormond Singularity is the goal—and getting to it before the criminals do. I've only got six months to do it.'

'Do you know what it is—this Ormond Singularity thing?'

'All we know is that it's some ancient law due to be repealed on the date I was warned about already—midnight, December 31st of this year.'

'Otherwise you'll turn into a pumpkin?' she joked, in her familiar, mocking way. 'We can't have that!'

'No,' I agreed with a grin. 'I was told that I had to lie low and hide until that day passed,' I continued, 'although I'm not sure I've been very successful in doing that, by heading up the Most Wanted list!'

She giggled and shoved me softly. I shoved her back.

'So every day that passes,' I said, 'brings that date closer. And I still don't know what I'm looking for. Whatever it is, it's kind of encrypted in this double-key code. I don't know how a jewel and a riddle can fit together.'

'What a challenge!' she smiled, without her usual cool superiority. 'Let's take another look at the Riddle,' she said enthusiastically. 'You have it with you?'

She waited while I pulled out clothes and other stuff from my backpack until I reached the Riddle folder. I pulled it out of its plastic sleeve and cautiously handed it over to her. Immediately, she started reading aloud.

The Ormond Riddle

Eight are the Leaves on my Ladyes Grace

Fayre sits the Rounde of my Ladyes Face

Thirteen Teares from the Sunnes grate Doore

Make right to treadde in Gules on the Floore

But adde One in for the Queenes fayre Sinne

Then alle shall be tolde and the Yifte unfold

As she read it, I felt even closer to understanding it. In my imagination, I started to get a misty picture of a queen walking across the floor, weeping. Why only thirteen tears? The mysterious image of the sad queen haunted me. What could it mean?

'Oriana mustn't have taken a copy of it,' Winter said, looking up from the Riddle. 'Otherwise she wouldn't be hunting you down to get it back, right?'

'Yeah, I guess.'

'I get a picture,' she said, 'in my imagination, of this lady, a queen, sitting in the garden weeping. Then she gets up and walks around and does something—fayre Sinne, whatever that is. And if you put all the pieces together properly, "all shall be told" and "something will unfold". The mystery will be revealed.'

'We're totally stuffed without the last two lines.'

'But the Jewel might help us with the Riddle. If they're part of the double-key code, then they must throw light on each other. We need to get hold of the Jewel.'

'I know,' I said. 'It belongs to my family, and I'm pretty sure it belonged to Dad before it was stolen from us, by Sligo. I want it back. I need your help, Winter,' I said. 'I have to get it from him. I need to know where he lives.'

'Leave it with me,' said Winter. 'I'll get you the information you need. I'll find a way to get inside.'

I wasn't so sure. But at least she had offered to help.

5:16 pm

The ring of Winter's phone interrupted us.

'Oh, no, it's Sligo!' she said, looking down at the screen.

I ran to the front window and looked out. I could see a man's figure coming up the top of the stairs, holding a phone to his ear!

'He's here! Coming up the stairs!' I said, grabbing my stuff and searching for an escape. 'So much for notice!'

Winter's worried face glared back at me. 'Quick, get out!' she urged.

I had no choice but to leave via the main building of flats. While Sligo was looking in the other direction I slipped out and raced across the roof to a doorway that led inside to the top floor. Ahead of me I could see the top of an internal staircase. I started taking the internal stairs two at a time, desperate to get down and out to the street as fast as possible.

24 JUNE

191 days to go . . .

5 Enid Parade, Crystal Beach

10:20 am

A few days had passed since I left Winter behind in her flat. When I told Boges about what happened there with Sligo showing up, I was relieved he didn't say, 'Told you so'.

No matter how hard I tried, I couldn't get her out of my mind. I tried to concentrate on the Riddle, which I knew off by heart now, but I always heard it in my head in Winter's voice.

I pounced on my phone when I saw Winter was ringing.

'I have Sligo's address for you,' she said.

'OK,' I said, 'Um, thanks.'

'Cal, I thought you'd be a little more excited than that! Hang on, you don't think I knew Sligo was coming to see me the other day, do you?' she asked, her friendly voice suddenly incredulous.

'How come you kept looking out the window?' I asked.

'You *do* think that! Cal, it's just a habit! I'm always on the lookout. I never feel completely relaxed! I would never do anything to put you in danger; you're my friend . . . aren't you?'

Winter paused and took a deep breath before continuing.

'You don't trust me,' she said, 'and I don't blame you. I have been unreliable. But I don't trust anyone or anything either. I don't even trust myself . . .'

Her voice cracked on the last few words. Miss Cool had lost her 'cool' and was crying. And this time, it was over something *I'd* said.

I felt really bad she was upset, but I kinda felt good at the same time, I guess because it sounded like she cared about what I thought of her. I didn't know what to say.

'I'm sorry,' she whispered.

And then she was gone. She'd hung up.

I'd been too hard on her. I never really believed she'd set me up, I was just letting her think that.

When my phone rang again, I snatched it, hoping it was Winter again, so that I could smooth everything over, check she was OK, and get the address, but it was Boges.

'Dude! I've got that address for you! I know where Sligo lives.'

'What? How did you get that?'

'I made a deal with Jamie. We started chatting again the other night and he cut me some slack on the cash he wanted. Instead I'm going to hook him up with a laptop and webcam, so he can keep in touch with his six-year-old daughter better—she lives interstate with his ex-wife or something.'

'Man, you rock! That is awesome!'

'I know!'

I grabbed a pen and noted down the address as Boges gave it to me.

'Great work!' I said.

'Hold the congratulations, my man. The address was not the only problem we faced.'

'What else?'

'The safe . . . Apparently it's the type that has a combination lock—you know, like the little safes in hotel rooms. Sounds like Sligo doesn't trust the modern ones, but anyway, you need to know the right numbers to press before the door will open. But without the right numbers, you'd need a bomb to open it.'

He paused for a moment before speaking again. 'I think we both know what's in that safe. But I think we need to know how to get into it before we go busting into the house.'

'OK. OK. I'll think of something. Call you back soon.'

11:11 am

I checked how I looked in the bathroom. I put the nerdy glasses on again and hurried downstairs and out of the house, keeping out of sight of the neighbours.

The wind blew cold under a grey sky. I hurried to the city, keeping my hoodie nice and high around my face so that very little of my features showed. Along the way I pulled the day's newspaper out from a rubbish bin, and bought two bacon and egg rolls from a takeaway shop.

I slipped through a gap in the wire fence at the disused railway yards. I kept my head down even though no-one was around. I couldn't be too careful near Repro's home.

Repro's Lair

12:39 pm

I looked around to make doubly sure no-one was following or watching me. I stood close to the three tall, metal cabinets leaning against the wall of rock. I leaned through the half open door of the central one and knocked hard inside it.

'Repro! It's me, Cal! I have the newspaper and a hot lunch for you! How about you let me in?'

Nothing happened. I tried again, banging harder on the cabinet's back wall.

But there was no response. I knocked more urgently. I had an idea that I hoped would get me in faster.

'Please open up!' I remembered a word he had used when I first met him. 'The bluecoats!' I hissed through the crack. 'The bluecoats are after me!'

I pushed with all my strength against the back wall, and just at that moment Repro must have removed whatever was blocking the entrance. I tumbled in headfirst and the secret door snapped back into position behind me while I sprawled on the dusty floor of the lair.

'Just dropping in again, are you?' laughed Repro as I rolled around.

I climbed to my feet, brushed myself down and looked at my friend. He was in another shabby, dark green suit, his long arms sticking out at the wrists, the whole outfit set off by a brilliant yellow bow tie. The colours of the Ormond Jewel, I thought to myself, hoping it was a good sign. He shook my hand vigorously—his own hands were in red woollen gloves with the fingertips cut out—before fetching the newspaper that had been sent sprawling across the room. I pulled the rolls out from under my hoodie, hoping they weren't too squashed.

'This is all very well,' he said, putting the food on the table and the newspaper on a shelf behind him, 'but I'm still waiting for my pay from the last job I did for you.'

With his thin hair brushed neatly across his scalp, and his possum eyes staring at me, he reminded me of some creature from another world—which in a way he kind of was.

'I'm a bit short of money at the moment,' I said, 'but I have a deal to suggest.'

Repro rolled his luminous eyes. 'You'd better sit down,' he said, 'and tell me all about it. But if it's a job like the other one, well, I'll be whistling for my pay.' He pulled out one of his rickety old chairs. 'I've heard all sorts of things about you, my boy. On the radio, on the telly, in the papers. You're everywhere! Did you really steal a jet and crash it?'

I dragged the old chair closer to me, ducked the row of washing, and sat down. We started eating lunch and I filled him in on some of my adventures, while he sipped loudly on his cup of tea. Repro was particularly interested in the flight of the Orca, and the fact that I'd walked away from crash-landing it.

'But now,' I said as he slurped the last of his tea, 'I've gotta get the Ormond Jewel back. And to do that, I need to get into a safe.'

'A combination safe?' asked Repro, his fingers already twitching, crumpling the paper bag from his roll into a tight ball.

'Yep,' I said looking down at my roll—I still had more than half of it left.

'Who owns it?' he said while carefully taking aim to toss the rubbish into a basket near the bathroom sink.

'Vulkan Sligo.'

These two words threw Repro completely off his target; the paper bag hit the wall, then rolled back across the floor.

'Too dangerous, too dangerous,' he said, shaking his head. 'Vulkan Sligo is not a nice man.'

'You don't need to tell me that,' I said, leaning closer to him, 'but you said a while back how you had a special gift, how you could feel the numbers used in combination safes.'

'Yes, yes,' said Repro, but he was shaking his head at the same time. 'I used to make a lot of money that way. Honestly, of course.'

My safe-cracking friend glanced approvingly at his long, slender fingers as he flexed them.

'Of course,' I said. 'The Jewel was stolen from us. It belongs to my family, not Sligo.'

'But you don't even know for sure if he has it?'

'Yes. Well, no, but . . . I'm almost one hundred per cent sure he's the one who pinched it.'

Repro rolled his eyes again, and sat back in his chair, unimpressed. I put my unfinished roll back in its bag—I'd lost my appetite. I understood why he wouldn't want to be involved, but I really needed his help.

'Can I at least get some more track detonators off you then?' I asked, hoping this visit wouldn't turn out to be a complete waste of time.

'Detonators aren't what you need. Take them, if you like,' he said, pointing to a tin on top of one of his book towers nearby. 'But you don't want to be making that kind of a bang when you're trying to silently break into someone's safe.'

He was right, but I took the tin anyway. It was heavy, about the size of a lunch box, and inside were four small detonators. They hardly needed a container of that size, but I figured it would give them some protection in my backpack.

'And you really don't want to make a bang like that,' added Repro, 'when you're not even sure what you want is in the safe.'

'I've gotta find out. If I can get you into Sligo's place, do you think you could feel the numbers and get the safe open? It'd be awesome if you wanted to help me, but if not . . . then I'll have to figure out something else.'

He lengthened his neck and straightened his bow tie. 'I don't *think* I could get it open, I *know* I could get it open.' He rubbed his fingers together and his eyes started sparkling. 'Wonder what else is sitting there in that big safe, eh?'

'So does that mean it's a deal?' I asked, holding my breath.

Repro stretched his hands out in front of him then clasped them together, cracking his knuckles loudly. I waited, tensely, hoping for him to swing one of his hands out to shake mine once more.

But it didn't happen.

Instead, my friend's face fell as he spoke. 'Sligo is a very dangerous man to have as an enemy. Too dangerous, I'm afraid.'

3:41 pm

On the cold walk back along Enid Parade the disappointment I was feeling was as frosty as the wind blowing in from the rolling, grey ocean. It was hopeless. Without Repro we had no chance of getting into that safe. And how were we going to get into Vulkan Sligo's house anyway, let alone find the chance for Repro—if he changed his mind—to have a go at the combination?

I must have been crazy to even think like this.

25 JUNE

190 days to go . . .

5 Enid Parade, Crystal Beach

5:26 pm

Sitting on the floor of the mansion, I was surrounded by Dad's drawings. The Riddle teased me with its cryptic words. I was still brooding over how to get access to Sligo's safe, when my mobile rang. It was Winter.

'Before you say anything,' she said, 'I just need you to believe something.'

'What's that?' I asked, wary.

'I did not know that Sligo was on his way up the other day. He said he was just calling in to say hi. He's only shown up like that once before—without ringing me first—to make sure I was with Miss Sparks, my tutor. Tell me you believe me, Cal. It's really important to me that you do.'

'Why should you care whether I trust you or not?'

'Because you're the only person who can understand what I'm going through,' she said passionately. 'Because we're alike—we're both on the outer. Because I already feel so different from everyone else in the world, if you won't trust me, then I'll feel even more alone.'

She'd hit a nerve in me. I knew what she meant.

'I feel that, too—most of the time,' I admitted.

'See?' Her voice was more urgent now. 'That's what I mean. We need to be friends—good friends—because we both get it. We don't have to put on an act for each other.'

'OK.'

'OK—what? Say it. Say you believe me—that I didn't know Vulkan was on his way.'

'I believe you didn't know that he was on his way,' I said, finally. 'I trust you.'

I never really thought that she'd set me up. She'd had loads of chances to dob me in, and hadn't. And without her, I may not have made it out of Leechwood Lodge. She had taken a serious risk, put herself in danger, to help me escape that place.

'Thanks,' she said, the relief in her voice obvious. 'That means everything to me.'

My heart was racing, as if I'd been running,

so I didn't hear what she said next.

'What was that?' I asked. 'What did you just say?'

'That I can help you with what you need,' she repeated.

'I already have Sligo's new address,' I said. 'Never mind how.'

'There's still something you don't have.'

'What's that?'

'How to get inside. How to get past security. I can look after that. I can get you inside.'

'How?' I asked, curiosity getting the better of me.

'Here's the plan,' she said. I listened while she outlined what she intended to do. Winter was proving again to be a good person to have on my side.

6:01 pm

Now I had access to Sligo's place, there was only one missing piece. I had to convince Repro to help. We had the address and a way in, but we needed magic fingers to get that safe open.

We had a real chance at retrieving the Ormond Jewel, as long as Winter was telling the truth. If she wasn't, I was walking straight into a trap.

Repro's Lair

7:12 pm

'What is it now?' Repro hissed from behind the back of the filing cabinet. 'You're going to blow my cover one day!'

I took a deep breath. 'I know I haven't paid you in full for the last job we did together, when I said I would. And I can't pay you for the job I want your help with, now. But I know you're a good man, and one day, when I've uncovered this mystery that my dad started investigating, I'm sure I'll be able to repay you very well.' I hoped I was telling my friend the truth! 'Until then, all I can do is ask you again—please help me.'

29 JUNE

186 days to go . . .

Raw Prawn Café

3:20 pm

Sligo was living in a semi-industrial area with a few vacant blocks of land that looked like they were waiting for residential development. I sat anxiously at a table outside the café Winter and I had agreed to meet at. She'd given me the name of a place that was apparently within sight of Sligo's house.

I hadn't told Boges what we were up to. I figured he might think I was crazy, allowing Winter to get me into Sligo's house. He seemed to trust her heaps more than he did at first, but he still didn't sound entirely sure about her. And I knew what he thought of me getting closer to a murderous criminal.

My eyes scanned up and down the street, until I saw Winter walking along on the other side of the road. She saw me in the café and hurried over. Little sparkles flashed in her wind-blown hair.

'Is your friend coming?'

'I hope so,' I said, uncomfortably. If he didn't show, we were stuffed.

Winter ordered three hot chocolates, which boosted my faith in Repro coming. If *she* believed he would show up, then so should I.

Moments later I saw him beyond the hedge that bordered the café. He was dressed in a drover's raincoat and wearing a Sherlock Holmes-style hat. Great, I thought. How to look inconspicuous. All he needed now was the old-fashioned pipe.

I got the introductions out of the way and was relieved that Winter didn't seem at all phased by Repro's peculiar appearance.

'Maybe you could lose that hat?' I suggested.

'Keeps the brain warm,' he said with a crack of his knuckles.

'And the ears,' Winter added, leaning towards him to tug at one of the sides. 'OK, listen up. Sligo's out at the moment, talking to the city council about some big party he wants to put on towards the end of the year. I'm hoping he'll stay on and have a drink with the councillors. He's having some landscape gardening done in the next few days and he wants to be here later when the nursery comes to deliver the plants and stuff. So basically, what I'm saying is that we have a small gap now.'

Our drinks arrived and Winter stopped talking.

'But Sligo could return at any time,' I said, once the waiter had moved on.

She nodded.

'OK, well, we'd better move. Have you got your story worked out?' I asked.

'Of course I do! What, worried about me, are you Cal? How sweet!' Winter's teasing smile sent shivers up my spine. 'Didn't you know I'm madly keen to get a car? Now I'm sixteen I can start learning, so I think Sligo should buy me one! At least, that's what I'm going to tell Max.'

'Who's Max? Are there more guys working for Sligo?'

'Well yeah—Bruno and Zombrovski are his top guns, but he has loads of people in his "employment". Probably most of them owe him something. Anyway, Max is at the house right now. He's a rev-head and it won't take much to get him distracted, talking about cars. I've known him for years, and he's one of the better ones, unless you cross him that is. I definitely wouldn't want to be on his bad side. So, if that meets your approval, Cal, I should get going!'

It sounded like a solid plan so we didn't waste any more time. Repro and I waited in the café, watching as Winter walked purposefully across the road, up the street, and up to the front door of Sligo's new residence. It was a huge, modern building, dark grey in colour, with a wraparound balcony on the first level overlooking the bottom floor. It could easily have been confused as an office building. In the surrounding grounds, landscape planning was marked out by piles of dirt and timber logs.

Winter seemed to press on an intercom, and after a few moments the door opened and she disappeared inside.

'What now?' asked Repro.

'I guess we wait for her signal,' I said. I was feeling totally psyched and pumped—ready for anything, every nerve twitching and jumping, and every muscle ready to pounce. The seconds dragged by.

I almost jumped when the front door opened again, and there was the small, distant figure of Winter Frey, beckoning us urgently.

I raced over the road with Repro close behind me. I was relieved to see he'd taken off his deerstalker hat.

'Quickly!' Winter hissed as the two of us hurried through the front door. 'Go straight up the stairs and into the first room on your right. It's not locked.'

Somewhere in the house I could hear a man talking on a phone. Winter saw my alarm. 'Do as I say,' she said. 'You two get upstairs. I can deal with this guy for a while. He's buying it so far. He's even started calling around to see if he can hook me up with a bargain!' She giggled before looking at Repro seriously. 'How long will it take?'

Repro looked at his fingers, turning them over to examine his nails.

'These are the hands of an artist,' he said. 'They feel numbers. That takes time. Like all great art.'

I grabbed his skinny arm. 'Come on!'

We ran stealthily up the stairs. At the top of the landing, I saw the door to the room Winter had spoken of. I pushed it and good as her word, it opened. We crept in.

Apart from the red curtains to the side of the long, tinted sliding doors, and the big black desk, everything was a dark grey: the carpet, the big chair behind the desk, and the safe.

'There it is,' I whispered. The safe recessed into the wall in the left-hand corner of the room. It must have weighed a tonne! The door had only two features: a metal handle and a dial in the centre that was a bit like the temperature knob on an oven. Repro stood in front of the forbidding door, rubbing his long thin fingers with glee, locking and interlocking them, bending and flexing them, ready for action.

'Ooh, lovely!' he exclaimed. 'Haven't seen one of these big tin cans for a while! It's just like the old days when I was a legend in the city. Let me at it!'

I watched as he flexed his skinny fingers one last time then dropped to his knees in front of the safe.

I hurried to the red curtains and carefully looked around them. What if Sligo refused to stay back for a drink or two and returned before Repro had finished? I could only hope that his meeting with the councillors would delay him long enough for Repro to crack the safe with his unusual skill.

4:09 pm

The minutes ticked by.

'How's it going?' I asked Repro, who squatted in front of the safe, twisting the combination dial first one way, then another. 'Any moment now,' I reminded him, 'Sligo could return. You've got to move faster!'

Repro turned around with a sad, even hurt

expression on his face. 'I'm a safe master! You can't hurry someone like me in this work. It's a very delicate operation. Just let me do what I need to do.'

I hurried back over from the window and checked out the contents of the desk, looking through the papers on top, pulling out the drawers underneath and flipping through anything I found.

'How are you going?' I asked anxiously, a few minutes later. 'How much longer will this take?'

Repro ignored me. He was intent on his job; his head was turned away from the dial on the safe, listening and feeling as he tested combinations of numbers. He moved the dial gently in one direction and then the other, his long fingers moving like spider legs.

'Ha! I got one!' he cried softly.

'One? All this time and you've only got one? How many are there?' I was careful not to raise my voice too much so the guy downstairs wouldn't hear us.

'Could be four, or even eight. Just depends.'

'Eight? And you've only just got one?'

He waved his hand at me as if to tell me to shut up.

Anxiety twisted my stomach into knots. I

knew too well what Sligo could do to us if we were caught. I was especially worried about Winter—I wondered how long her ruse would hold up. I couldn't keep still, pacing from the safe to the window again, looking beyond the piles of dirt at the front of the house to the street.

A large truck was approaching, its flat tray filled with plants in pots, from small shrubs right up to young palm trees that swayed as the vehicle turned into the front garden. The landscaping people were here.

'Ah! There's number two!' said Repro, looking over at me. 'See? I told you I had a gift. That's two done now!'

My mobile rang on the vibrate setting and I pulled it out. 'Yes?'

'I'm still downstairs,' Winter whispered. 'Sligo just rang Max. The meeting at the council is finished. He's on his way home—you don't have much more time. Are you almost done?'

'No! He's only just begun! He's just found the second number out of a possible eight!'

'Please just hurry! He can't find out I let you in, Cal!'

I put the phone down and said, 'Repro, that was Winter. Sligo's on his way. Please hurry!'

Repro didn't answer, just gave a slight nod to

acknowledge I'd spoken. He was crouched like some crazy overgrown goblin, muttering away, fingers flying.

4:38 pm

My chest was pounding; I was sweating—I couldn't keep still. The landscape gardening truck was parked out front, and the driver was sitting on several stacked bags of soil mix, talking on his phone. No doubt he was awaiting instructions as to where to put the plants lining the back of his truck. Waiting for Sligo.

Unless the traffic was really heavy, it wouldn't take Sligo that long to get back here. So much time had elapsed already.

'Please hurry!' I begged the frantic figure in front of the safe.

I wished I hadn't spoken because Repro stopped what he was doing and slowly stood up, turning to face me.

'If you don't stop hassling me, kid, you can come and do it yourself!'

'OK, OK. I won't hassle you. But please, please just get on with it!'

'What do you think I've been doing here so far? Eh?'

'OK! Just do it!'

4:45 pm

Now I jiggled with anxiety, constantly peering through the glass down to the front entrance, dreading the sight of Sligo's black Subaru.

'How are you going, Repro?' I asked in what I hoped was a calm voice. He turned to me, his fingers still gripping the dial.

'I keep running through them and there are several that are easier to turn than the others, but I think I've almost got it. I just scored the third digit, and now I think I only have to find two more.'

Two? We didn't have time for him to find two more! This whole thing was turning out to be impossible. He could spend all night on it and still not get the right combination.

I ran my hands through my hair in frustration, when I saw something that made my blood run cold.

But before I could say anything, Repro yelled in triumph.

'Four! I have four of them! I've still got it! These are magic fingers here, my boy! Just one more to go!'

'You'd better find the fifth one fast!' I said, watching the black Subaru pull up out front. 'We've got company!'

Repro nodded and played the combination

dial like a delicate instrument.

Hurry up! I screamed inside, starting to panic about how we were going to get out of this house with Sligo hanging around out the front. If we were caught in the act of breaking into Sligo's safe, there was no way we'd get out alive.

'I think I've got it,' Repro muttered. 'I'm pretty sure it's 4-8-7-3 plus one more. Just feeling around for the last one now—I think it could be—'

His voice trailed off as he spun the dial around.

'Sligo has Red Singlet with him. They're coming up to the front door!' I hissed.

I could hear their voices downstairs near the front entrance. I prayed that Winter was still there and that her story would delay Sligo long enough to prevent him from coming upstairs and finding us.

'Got it! I've got the last number!' whispered Repro gleefully. 'It's a 6!'

I ran over to watch as Repro clicked in the final number, then swung the handle. With a soft whine, the heavy door opened. I directed the desk light into the dark interior of the safe and peered over Repro's shoulder.

My jaw dropped. I was immobilised.

'Holy hallucinating hamsters!' breathed Repro reverently. 'Would you look at that!'

What we were gazing at was without a doubt the most awesome thing I had ever seen! Illuminated in the light, and set in elaborate shining gold, the huge emerald—'big as a pigeon's egg', just as it had been described—glowed the deepest green while the rubies winked red fire between the alternating pearls. At the bottom of the oval of gold and jewels hung a pearl drop.

'The Ormond Jewel,' I breathed.

4:55 pm

The proximity of Vulkan Sligo's voice broke the spell cast on us by the amazing Jewel. I could never forget that voice. That was the voice that had barked the order to throw me into the oil tank to drown only a few months ago. Sligo was downstairs, but he could come up and walk in on us at any second.

I snatched up the Ormond Jewel, and at the same time, Repro grabbed a wad of cash that was sitting beside it, wrapped with a rubber band. He stuffed the cash into his pocket, and I stuffed the Jewel down in the bottom of my backpack after sneaking a quick peek at the picture of the Queen inside. Just as I was about to turn and run, a large colour photo lying on the floor of the safe caught my eye.

In it was Winter with a frangipani in her

streaming hair, wearing an amazing silver dress. I paused for crucial seconds. My heart lurched when I spotted what else she was wearing in the photo . . .

Something that freaked me out completely!

The Ormond Jewel!

How could she? Had she known about it all along? It didn't make sense! I thought of her downstairs right this minute—if she was even there any more—allegedly diverting the attention of one of Sligo's minders. She seemed to be helping us but after what I had just seen . . . Would I ever know whose team she was really playing on?

I snatched the picture up and examined it closely. It had a grainy texture, making it look like it had been enlarged. Winter's eyes seemed to gaze right into mine.

'No time for looking at pretty girls,' Repro's voice interrupted me. 'I thought you said we were in *a bit of a rush*?' he quipped.

I chucked the photo back into the safe and Repro and I darted through the sliding doors and out onto the balcony that overlooked the front of the building. I peered over to see if there was a way to climb down to the ground a few metres below, where the nursery truck was parked.

The voices from downstairs became louder. Winter was still there—she sounded distressed. Sligo was yelling. And coming closer! He must have realised something was up! Footsteps pounded up the staircase—any second now and they'd burst in on us.

'We have to jump!' I urged Repro. I hoped if we took our chances and jumped onto the back of the truck beneath, that the thick foliage and soft soil of the potted plants and palms would cushion our fall. I also hoped we wouldn't be impaled on the stakes keeping a few palms straight, in position.

I went first, my backpack strapped on tight. I edged over the balcony railing and dangled down as close to the ground as I could get.

Here goes! I thought.

I let go and moments later I landed heavily, half on my side, smashing into several prickly potted shrubs. Immediately Repro landed on top of me, winding me!

I gasped for breath and struggled to sit up. Repro was already pushing aside the smashed plants, climbing to the edge of the tray.

'What are you doing?' I called as he jumped to the ground. 'Where are you going?'

'I'm outta here!' he shouted, before disappearing.

I couldn't believe it. He was bailing out on me! I knew Repro was a loner, but I never thought he would leave me on my own!

'There he is! Somebody grab him! You scumbag! You thief!' Sligo yelled down from the balcony.

One of Sligo's goons would be racing out the front door, grabbing me and hauling me off the truck in seconds.

I struggled to free myself, and my backpack containing the precious Jewel, which had become entangled with the long branches of a palm tree.

With a thrill of fear, I saw the front door swing open, and Bruno in his red singlet charged out. He was just metres away. Desperately, I looked for an escape, but there was nothing I could do, I was a goner!

Suddenly, the truck lurched forward, nearly throwing me off the back! With its wheels spinning then digging into the dirt, the truck recklessly reversed off Sligo's property and into the street, almost mowing down Bruno in the process. I couldn't look, I was bracing myself for a collision with the oncoming traffic. I heard the screech of brakes, horns blaring, and someone swearing, but the collision never came. Instead the truck kept reversing until finally it lurched forward again, roaring through the gears as I clung on for my life. Half the load of plants up-ended and catapulted past me, off the back of the truck, crashing and shattering onto the road behind us.

Grabbing onto the sides, I peered through the palm leaves to the cabin window to see who had saved me.

It was Repro! He hadn't abandoned me after all!

He spotted me in the rear-vision mirror, and wriggled the fingers on his left hand in the air for me to see.

'Not just good for getting safes open!' he shouted. 'Also brilliant at getting cars started!'

5:15 pm

As the speed of the truck settled down, and with no sign of any pursuers, I got my breath back again. I lay against some crushed pot plants and closed my eyes for a moment. We'd gotten away with the Ormond Jewel!

I took the Jewel out of my backpack and held it in my hands, rocking with the movement of the truck, fascinated again by its glowing presence. Just for a moment, I didn't care where we were going—I didn't care where Repro was driving us or that Sligo and Bruno might be in hot pursuit. In my hands I had the Ormond Jewel; in my backpack I had the Ormond Riddle. A huge surge of wild and triumphant energy raced through my body.

Now I had both parts of the double-key code!

I turned the Jewel over in my hand and for the first time really looked at the back of it. My eyes widened with surprise. In spite of the dangerous situation I was in I saw something on the back of it that caused another thrill of excitement to run through me. A connection with Dad's drawings! I tucked it safely back into my bag and pulled out my phone.

'Guess what I've got?' I said, when Boges answered.

'I hope it's not contagious,' he joked. 'Where the heck are you? Sounds like you're in a wind tunnel!'

'Almost–I'm in the middle of a kind of moving jungle right now,' I said, brushing a palm leaf out of my face. 'Boges! I've got it! I've got the Ormond Jewel!'

'What? When? How?' he asked with increasing excitement.

I glanced up and the triumph energising me chilled. Through the remaining palm leaves I saw the black Subaru coming after us in the distance. Only two other cars sat between us, and the Subaru was already overtaking the first car. 'Hang on, Boges. There's a critical emergency happening!'

I bashed on the back of the cabin, yelling. 'Sligo's on us! Drive faster!'

I gripped the sides of the truck as Repro stepped on it. We surged forward, sending even more potted trees tumbling off the back. I watched as a big one crashed to the road, forcing the car travelling behind us to swerve dangerously to avoid it. The black Subaru had to dodge it too.

'Did I just hear you right?!' Boges shouted down the line. 'Sligo's after you? Where are you?' he repeated.

'Somewhere heading south, on the back of a truck. Sligo is gaining fast!'

I rapped on the back window again. 'Put your foot down, Repro!' I yelled. He obliged. The truck lurched faster along the road, sending another potted palm over the side.

'Boges,' I yelled into my phone, 'it's the most beautiful, amazing, awesome thing you ever saw!'

'Dude! I can't believe you've got it! But are you gonna make it away from Sligo or what?'

'I don't know, man!' I said, rocking and rolling around in soil, crushed foliage and broken clay pots. I held on as well as I could. The Subaru was gaining. Soon it would be right behind us.

'How'd you do it?' Boges asked.

'Winter acted as a decoy while Repro worked his skill to get the Jewel out of the safe.'

'Why didn't you let me know this was going down? I could have helped!'

'Boges, it kind of just happened like that,' I said. 'Sorry–'

'And putting all that trust in Winter,' Boges interrupted. 'But I guess she got you in and out in one piece! And you have the Jewel!'

I pictured the photo I found in the safe of Winter wearing the Jewel. I still wasn't sure what to make of it. But, he was right, we were out, I had the Jewel, and now we had to get away from the Subaru.

'Boges there's something else!' I said, forgetting Winter for a moment. 'There's a rose on the back of it! And in Dad's drawing there's a rose that the boy is holding! Something matches up here!'

The roses weren't identical, but they were roses. Two seemingly unrelated objects–the drawing made by my dad, and this amazing piece of jewellery, hundreds of years old, suddenly came together.

Repro made a fast, violent turn on the road and I fell forward. When I regained my balance, I grabbed up my mobile again.

'You still there, Boges?' I asked.

'You bet your life I am!'

'There's this catch on one side of the Jewel,' I continued, 'and when you open it—it's like a big locket—there's this picture of Queen Elizabeth I, just like Bartholomew's book described!'

'Dude, that is wild! All the secret doors are opening! But where are you heading? Are you going to get away OK?'

'Hope so! We're headed south along the coast, so we'll lose them somewhere near the water.'

Sligo's car had overtaken the other car that was behind us and was only about twenty metres away. I thumped on the back window, 'Faster, Repro! Faster!' then shouted down the line to Boges. 'I've got to go!'

5:31 pm

We were driving fast along the Southern Highway and the black Subaru was only a few car lengths behind us. On our left, across the stunted coastal vegetation, was the hazy ocean.

I dragged a couple of the remaining pot plants off the truck, throwing them down into the Subaru's path. They smashed on the bitumen in explosions of soil and clay, but the car skilfully swerved and weaved around them. Next I started firing the smaller pots. The car steamrolled over most of them, but one hit the target and bounded up the car's bonnet, cracking the windscreen. The impact stalled the Subaru for a few seconds, but then it was back on track with a vengeance.

I'd gone through too much to lose the Jewel and the Riddle. I looked around, wondering how I could hide them. I saw a toolbox in the tray behind the cabin window and pounced on it, snatching up a roll of wide, grey electrical tape which had been used to hold the palm trees to their stakes. Quickly, I dug the Ormond Jewel, the Riddle and my dad's drawings out of my backpack. I threw away the plastic folder, tore a piece of thin, black plastic off a sheet that had been covering part of the soil, wrapped everything up really tight, then taped the package carefully to the very bottom of my bag. It wasn't perfect but it was the best I could do. I just hoped no-one would catch up with us and have a reason to check my bag too closely.

I had to plan a way out. We didn't have much time—Sligo's Subaru was so close behind us, and anywhere we pulled over or turned off would be plain for him to see. Our only chance was to ditch the truck and make a dash for it, losing ourselves in the scrub. I didn't know where we were heading, and apart from bashing on the window and yelling to Repro to drive faster, I couldn't really communicate a plan with him, unless we stopped.

Suddenly, the truck veered wildly off the road, across the shoulder and through some straggly bushes.

The black Subaru shot right past the spot where Repro had swung off the road like some driving champion. I cheered wildly, and thumped the cabin excitedly, before hunkering down in the back again. I knew we only had seconds before they would turn around and chase after us.

I clung on as we jolted and jumped our way right over the bushes and into a cleared area that looked like it might have once been a group of playing fields, now neglected and overgrown.

But then I saw where we were headed—we were going to be snookered! 'What's happening?' I yelled, spotting what looked like a large kite, tilting in the wind. 'There's a cliff straight ahead of us—this is not a good place to stop!'

The truck slowed down and then stopped completely. I jumped off the back and ran around to the driver's door.

Repro climbed out of the cabin, opening his spooky hands wide in a helpless gesture. He shrugged. 'We've got to make it on foot now! Follow me!'

The cover of the low coastal scrub would hardly hide us. I pointed to the cliff that was overlooking the ocean. 'But we need to go in that direction!'

With a prickling of fear, I swung round, hearing another vehicle. The Subaru was turning off the road; in a few moments it would be here. Repro had already taken off and was running back towards the bushes near the road. I wasn't fast enough to follow him that way. I looked around desperately. Maybe I could somehow climb down the cliff and hide somewhere under an overhang.

The black car was halfway across the cleared area. I didn't know what to do!

I took off towards the cliff. What I'd thought was a large kite near where we'd skidded to a halt was actually a hang-glider! I'd done a bit of hang-gliding with Dad before—we'd tried para-gliding *and* hang-gliding—and hoped I remembered how the harnessing straps worked as I raced over to it, preparing to use it as my getaway vehicle.

I could hear the Subaru speeding up behind me. Come on, Cal, I told myself. You've flown a *jet*. And you've walked away from a crash-landing!

I clipped myself in, relieved I didn't have too much trouble, grabbed the steering bar and ran at full tilt towards the cliff edge.

It was only after I'd already run too far to go back that I considered the possibility of crashing and falling to my death on the rocks below, or spinning out-of-control into the ocean, and that maybe this glider had some fatal damage and that's why it had been dumped.

I had to jump into thin air! Heart pounding with anxiety, my scrambling legs lifted off the ground and lurched as the hang-glider rose a metre or so in the air.

Beneath me a man emerged from behind some bushes, pulling up his trousers.

'Hey!' he yelled up at me. 'Get down from there! That's my glider! What do you think you're doing?' He must have been answering the call of nature in the privacy of the thick scrub near the cliff's edge.

'I'm just borrowing it!' I shouted down. Suddenly the wind swept me up and, as my stomach turned over, I felt myself caught up even higher. I was flying effortlessly and soundlessly, cruising on the updraught heading high into the air.

I clung onto the steering bar, and tilted it to the right. Big mistake! The steering was very sensitive and the glider fell sharply. For a moment I thought I was going to fall straight down. But in seconds the currents picked me up again and I soared off to the left, this time remembering that this fragile craft, although so totally different to the Ormond Orca, was built to fly and was equally sensitive to steering directions.

As I hung there in my harness with the wind-rush in my ears and hair, I was aware of distant, barely-audible curses and shouts behind me. Carefully, I turned my head and looked behind me to see the Subaru almost at the cliff's edge. Sligo and Bruno stood beside it, screaming with rage. The sound of the wind and the roaring surf a hundred metres beneath me took the words out of their mouths. And the longer they stood there, shouting into the sky at me, the longer Repro had to get away.

I was free! I had escaped from Sligo once again! I had the Jewel and the Riddle safely in my backpack! Elation and exhilaration fizzed through my veins as I soared out over the sea. The freedom I felt as I rode on the updraught was miraculous. This must be how eagles and falcons feel as they sail on the wind. Carefully, I played around with the craft, shifting my body weight back so that the nose of the hang-glider lifted and I rose higher in the air.

Shifting my body weight forward caused the nose to go down and I found myself dropping towards the sea. I pulled back again and lifted the hang-glider higher—I didn't want to get into a stall.

I didn't have a crash helmet or goggles and I had to squint against the powerful wind rushing past me.

Below, I could see small fishing boats with flocks of seagulls swirling around them. The southerly was carrying me north, back towards the direction of the city. In the west, the sun had disappeared and the sky was turning pink and purple. I knew I needed to make landfall before it got too dark.

6:03 pm

The sky was darkening quickly. I needed to swing to the left, but tacking across the wind required gliding skills that I didn't have. I didn't want to oversteer and spear down into the sea, so, very lightly, I leaned into the steering bar. The hang-glider responded perfectly, softly turning towards land.

I was aiming for a cleared headland I could see a little further north, where some warm lights twinkled against the dusky twilight of the coast. The wind eased a lot as the headland came closer and closer. The lights I'd seen earlier turned out to be campfires, and now I could see a couple of groups of people and their tents. I hoped landing on the sand wouldn't be too rough.

I was losing altitude fast. I didn't want to mess up and land in the water–I hadn't forgotten the sharks in January. Again I gently shifted my weight to the left, into the steering bar, letting the hang-glider do the flying for me.

I was almost over the beach now, so I turned into the wind, preparing for landing, and aimed for the soft sand before the straggly scrub began at the front of the headland. The beach was coming up at me fast and I tried to lift the nose but I'd left it too late. I battled to pull it up as I saw the ground rushing to meet me. The hang-glider was descending nose-first!

Just before impact I used all my strength to shift the glider and lift the nose, which sent us skidding across the sand, smoothly.

6:18 pm

'Wow, that was awesome!' came a voice from nearby.

A kid a few years younger than me had run over from a small campfire on the shore as I disentangled myself from the hang-glider. I crawled out and got to my feet. My legs were trembling but, at last, I was on firm ground again.

'Thanks,' I said. I looked around, my heart rate easing off. I shook my head to clear it. I'd landed the glider perfectly!

'You came down so fast,' commented the kid, 'I thought you were gonna crash it for sure!'

'Me too!' I admitted.

'Your hang-glider's sick,' said the kid. He looked hard at me. 'Do I know you from somewhere?'

I adjusted the straps on my backpack and hitched it higher between my shoulders.

'Don't think so. Where am I?'

'It's Zenith Beach!' said the kid, like I was crazy. I'd heard of Zenith Beach. It was a famous surfing beach, and I knew I was a long way from home—wherever that might be these days. 'You must have blown off course!' he added.

'Just a little bit,' I said as I began walking across the sand, aiming for the road beyond it. I could see the headlights of the cars climbing the winding road around the headland.

'Hey! What about your hang-glider?' he called after me.

I pictured the poor guy who owned it, shouting at me back at the cliff's edge . . . 'My friend will be around in an hour or two to collect it,' I shouted back.

6:35 pm

The road from Zenith Beach joined a highway north about a kilometre away and when I reached it, I messaged Boges.

heading back from zenith beach. talk soon?

The traffic flowed by steadily. But this time, I didn't want to hitchhike. I didn't want to take any unnecessary risks, especially with the treasures hidden in my backpack, so I just kept on walking. I was watching my back, making sure the black Subaru wasn't creeping up on me.

It got cold really quickly, and I wished Boges would get back to me. A message beeped on my mobile, but it wasn't from Boges.

It was a long message, from an anonymous sender. Puzzled, I headed away from the road and stopped to read it, sliding down to sit against a tree.

Still working through archives re: Ormond Singularity. Still seeking main body of legislation, but have found important codicil regarding eligibility of heir; must be aged 16 or above. If heir dies before 16th birthday, whatever benefits the Ormond Singularity might bring, reverts to next of kin in bloodline . . . He must go.

Someone had sent me a text about the Ormond Singularity. I scrolled back to find any details about the sender, but there was nothing.

If heir *dies?*

He must go?

My sixteenth birthday was only a month away—July 31st. Was I the heir the message was talking about? Heir to *what*? The Ormond Singularity? What did that mean? And who had sent this to me? I sat there wondering whether it was a warning or a threat.

I forwarded it to Boges, asking him to get back to me fast, and if he could track whoever had sent it. I re-pocketed my mobile and climbed to my feet. I had to get back to the city. I *had* to find out where this message had come from.

Back near the road I hunched down against the cold and kept walking. I was getting more and more desperate to see Boges and work out this bizarre message as well as put together the pieces of the double-key code. I'd decided earlier against hitchhiking, but impatience made me stick out my thumb as a couple of cars sped past me. I could hear a hotted-up car coming up behind me and the sound of the engine slowing raised my hopes. I stopped and turned to look and as I did, the slowed vehicle took off with a screech of tyres and an echo of wild yells from its passengers.

Although I knew they were just messing with me, I couldn't help feeling rattled by it, so I carried on walking, thinking my legs would have to be good enough to get me home.

As I walked on, those menacing words kept repeating in my mind. *Heir dies before 16th birthday . . . He must go . . .* I was so distracted that I didn't notice the police car pulling up beside me until it was too late. While I waited with sweaty palms for the cops to get out and approach me, I told myself: You're Ben Galloway and you weren't doing anything wrong.

Only one cop got out of the car. He was built like a footballer, with very short blond hair.

'OK, son. Got any ID on you?' he said.

'What's wrong, Officer?'

'Sergeant—Sergeant Roberts,' he said, taking the Ben Galloway travel pass from me, examining my face and my photo by the powerful light on the side of the police car.

'Constable, check this name and date of birth,' he called, spelling out the Ben Galloway details to his unseen partner behind the wheel. The two of us stood in silence as traffic whizzed past.

Finally, the constable called out, 'Bring him in, Sarge. There are a few questions outstanding for Ben Galloway.'

The sergeant opened the back door of the car and then reached for me, putting a firm hand on my back. He guided me into the vehicle. 'You were hitching for a ride, now you're in luck. Get in!'

I climbed in, completely defeated. I didn't know what sort of a record Ben Galloway had, aside from escaping a mental hospital. Either way, as Ben Galloway or Cal Ormond, I was clearly in big trouble. And I didn't think it would take long for the cops to work out who I really was.

I sat in the back, listening to the cops' conversation, trying to work out how I was going to get away from this situation—and all the time, five particular words from the anonymous text message haunted my mind: *heir dies before 16th birthday*.

The words felt ominous, like a curse. I clutched my backpack closely, feeling incredibly protective of what was mine. What was *staying* mine.

Southport Police Station

7:56 pm

Constable Cook, the driver, pulled into the small carpark beside the police station and backed into a car space. There was one other squad car there. The cops got me out, then led me through the back door of the station, which Sergeant Roberts swiped open with the ID card hanging round his neck. We passed through the corridors until we came to a small room that was similar to my living quarters at the clinic—sparse and cold. There was nothing in it except a table, three chairs and a large clock on the wall.

I knew they would want to see what was in my bag, and I couldn't let them get to it first. I decided I had to take charge and be brazen if I had any hope of keeping the Ormond Jewel a secret. Whether they knew who I was or not, they would not let a fifteen-year-old kid off if they found an ancient emerald hidden in his backpack. They'd instantly assume me to be a thief.

'I suppose you want to see what's in here,' I scoffed. 'We may as well get it out of the way.' I tipped up my bag and out spilled my clothes, radio, torch, chocolate bars . . . I even unrolled my sleeping-bag and rolled it up again.

The package held tightly to the inside of my bag, remaining a secret.

Roberts watched as I sifted through my pile of stuff in front of them. 'What's that?' he asked, grabbing the tin I'd taken from Repro's place.

The tin with the detonators! I'd completely forgotten about them! How was I going to explain this one?!

I watched with dread as he prised open the lid with a strong grip.

'Oh, gross!' he shouted, pushing the tin away from him.

'What is it?' asked Constable Cook, peering into the tin. But before he was even close enough to see what was in there he backed away, covering his nose. 'That's foul, buddy!'

I had to peer into it myself to see what they were talking about. As soon as I saw the paper bag package in there, I realised what had saved me—my bacon and egg roll leftovers! I'd shoved it in there before I left Repro's that day!

'Oh, I forgot about that,' I said with a shrug. 'Bacon and egg roll,' I admitted. 'Maybe four or five days old . . .' I quickly grabbed the tin and pressed the lid back down firmly on top of it, then crammed all of my things back into my bag.

Roberts grunted and put my backpack on a chair. 'OK, OK, Ben. Thanks for the show. I'll get this put away for you.'

'We'll return your stuff to you later,' added Cook. 'But for the time being you can cool your heels in here.'

They walked out and closed the door behind them.

30 JUNE

185 days to go . . .

5:18 am

Last night Cook and Roberts had been waiting on word from some other station on what to do with me, so they made the decision to hold me in a cell until further instruction. I started out confident, feeling awesome that the Jewel, the Riddle and Dad's drawings had remained unseen in my backpack, and thinking I'd find a way out. Somehow. But as the time in lock-up ticked by, so did my bravado.

I'd had scattered sleep. I couldn't stop thinking of the bizarre text message I'd received. People had been trying to take me out of the picture all year, but if someone was planning to make sure I didn't reach my sixteenth birthday, maybe I was safer in police custody. I hated thinking that, but I was completely over it. I knew that turning myself in would be like handing over everything I'd uncovered about the DMO to Sligo and Oriana. Our family would never be the same again.

I was trapped, no matter what side of the bars I was on.

6:32 am

During my restless sleep, flashes of the fire at 'Kilkenny' re-entered my mind. Some of Great-uncle Bartholomew's last words suddenly came back to me, fast, like a slap across the face: *I want to tell you something. The kidnapping of those babies . . . that you read about. One of them . . . one of them . . . is you . . . you . . . you have to go now.*

Me? Was he trying to say that one of them was me? Or was he cut short of what he really wanted to say? The newspaper clipping about the missing baby mystery had completely disappeared from my memory, until now. Unfortunately the solicitor's name hadn't come back with it.

I felt in my gut that there was a pretty serious reason for Bart to have saved that article. It *must* have been important to him. To our family. I felt like something else, something really bad, must have happened that I didn't know about. A secret that no-one wanted me knowing. Mum had mentioned at the hospital something from my past that she seemed to think was big enough to have made me . . . go psycho. Would I ever find out?

10:02 am

I woke up with a start, lifting my head from the bed.

Roberts came in with a cup of coffee and a sandwich. 'Room service,' he joked, putting the food on a tray in front of me. I rubbed my eyes and attempted to wake up properly.

'We've found out some very interesting things about you, Ben,' he said. 'We want to ask you a few questions. I'll be back when Cook gets in.'

He left me alone again. I was starving and quickly ate the food and guzzled the coffee.

When Roberts returned, he led me down the corridor to a large, open-plan office with several empty desks. The place was almost deserted. He pushed me towards his desk and I noticed that on the wall next to it was a board with the keys for the two squad cars. Under the board was a counter with a pile of phone books and my back-pack sitting on it.

'Please, sit down,' he said.

I did so.

Cook looked up from the desk he was sitting behind. 'I'm on the line to city headquarters,' he called to his partner. 'Now they want us to take him in there,' he said with a frustrated tone. 'Some new lead in the Spencer case is holding them up right now.' He smiled at me, menacingly. 'It's going to be a long, long day.'

Desperately, I looked around for some way of escape. With two cops between me and the door, there wasn't one. What I needed right now was something impossible—to get hold of an ID card and my backpack, grab a set of keys for a car, unlock the back door of the police station, and jump into one of the fast pursuit vehicles parked outside.

As if.

'Damn,' said Cook, putting the phone down and standing up. He took off his ID and hung it on a desk lamp. 'I was hoping to knock off on time today. Gotta pick up the in-laws from the airport at nine. But it looks like we've gotta take you into the city instead,' he said to me.

'You can do both,' said Roberts. 'We can't leave the station until after seven-thirty tonight, but if you drive, drop me and Galloway at headquarters, then you can continue on with the car. You should make it.'

Cook nodded.

'Sorry mate,' he said to me with another nod

of his head, 'but you're going back in the cell for awhile.'

7:45 pm

It wasn't until night that Roberts let me out of my cell. We were sitting back at the desks we were at earlier in the morning, waiting on Cook to finish up some paperwork.

Cook approached, with a tired sigh. Roberts lifted a set of keys marked '02' from the board, and jiggled them in his hand. I shifted in my seat and pointed to my backpack. Neither of them objected so I walked over and hoisted it up on my shoulder.

By thinking of the impossibility of what I needed to do, I'd actually rehearsed the moves of what happened next!

'Here,' Roberts called to Cook. 'Catch!'

In a split-second, I dived into the air, intercepted the car keys that were being tossed, snatched Cook's ID from the desk lamp, and was off before they'd even worked out what had happened! I raced down the corridor to the back door, swiped it open with the ID, and in three strides I was unlocking the second white Commodore, jumping into the driver's seat and turning the key in the ignition.

Roberts and Cook came racing out the back

door. But they were too late! I did a huge burnout and screeched out of the carpark, leaving the two cops running uselessly behind me. I yanked the seatbelt across me, then wrenched the steering wheel round, just like I used to when Dad would take me for driving lessons on the flat land behind Treachery Bay.

I knew I didn't have much time before an all-points bulletin would be issued for my arrest, and Southport 02—the car I'd nicked—would become the focus of every police car-chase in the city.

I recklessly sped down the road, aiming for the beach. I hoped that I could get lost down there. Meanwhile, I just had to concentrate on driving as fast as I could through the streets of the city, careening and swerving, listening to the distant sirens. I knew they'd have a helicopter in the area in no time and once I was spotted from the air, I was gone. The squad car radio was going crazy: every car in the area was being called in to hunt me down.

In the rear-vision mirror, I saw the headlights and the flashing red and blue lights behind me. I flattened my foot to the floor and Southport 02 leaped ahead. The seagulls swirling around the lights wheeled in fright as I screeched past them. I was heading for the green open space of the parkland near the jetty, just south of the beach. Beyond that were lanes with houses and fences and gardens—places I could possibly hide in if I had the chance to abandon the car.

I was running out of road so I veered to the left, towards the promenade. Southport 02 cleared the kerb with a crunch of metal and kept going, across the paved area south of the beach and onto the grass. Behind me three police cars copied my movements exactly. They were coming after me and they were catching up with me!

I screamed across the headland park. As I braked to avoid hitting the row of log seats running along the sea side of the park, I completely lost control of the car. The back-end swung around, ploughing up a wide fan of grass and soil through which I could see the headlights of three police cars charging for me. I jumped out and ran for my life down towards the wharf and jetty.

My mobile rang and I snatched it out of my pocket as I ran.

'Dude!' said Boges. 'Some weird stuff is going down. Where are you? We seriously need to talk.'

'Not now Boges! I can't talk!' I shouted—I was crazy to have answered it!

'But I've gotta tell you! Everything on the net about the Ormond Riddle has been deleted. That website's no longer there. I've been online all day trying to find out what happened to it. It's been deleted totally. I can't find any reference to it anywhere now! As for this anonymous text message–'

'Boges! I'll call you back!'

I hung up and ran all-out, thinking that the cops couldn't be far behind. I barely had time to think about what Boges had said. He was right about weird stuff going down, but there was nothing I could do about that just now. I put it out of my mind and ran harder.

I raced onto the jetty, thinking that if I dived in and swam underwater for a while, I would have a chance of escaping. It was dark. It'd be hard to spot me. A red and black jet ski, shining in the light at the end of the wharf, was just docking, idling as its owner leaned over to secure it to a mooring on the jetty. I had nothing to lose and so I jumped for it, knocking him out of the way and into the water.

'Sorry, mate!' I yelled, as I accelerated away, pulling the jet ski around his splashing body. 'No time to explain!'

A great slew of water fanned up in an arc around me!

The water was freezing. I was so pumped about getting away from the cops, with the Ormond

Jewel safely stashed in my backpack, that it was a while before I realised I had no idea where I was going. I kept the lights of the city to my left and continued speeding up the coast, the jet ski slapping against the light chop. Even though I was freezing and wind-chill made me even colder in my wet clothes, the excitement and triumph kept me going.

I told myself I should stay near to land. I couldn't see how much fuel I had and I sure didn't want to be stuck out at sea too far from the coast. Thoughts of sharks circled in my mind again, but I pushed them aside.

The strange, threatening words in the mysterious text message returned to me, reminding me of an announcement in the death columns: 'Heir dies before sixteenth birthday.' Now the Ormond Riddle reference had vanished from the web. Someone was seriously messing with my head.

The message had been sent to *me*. The message was *about* me. In another month I'd be sixteen—if I lived that long.

I was thinking it was about time I headed for the shore, when the sound of an approaching speedboat made me turn around.

I gulped in fear.

Bearing down on me, its lights shining brilliantly, was police boat *Stingray*. Despite the roar of the jet ski's engine, I could hear distorted shouting through a loud hailer.

'Police! Stop! Cal Ormond! Stop!'

They were calling my name! The Ben Galloway identity had been blown. Now the cops knew who they were really after!

My only chance was to lose myself among the shadowy boats in the harbour ahead. Turning the throttle full on, I sped towards it. I aimed for the busiest section near the marina where several yachts were under sail.

The water was choppy because of the wash from a ferry as well as a stiff, offshore breeze. The jet ski bobbed up and down, smacking back into the water as I rounded the point past the marina. Ahead of me, one of the large ferries that went from the city to the headland sounded its horn. Behind me, *Stingray* was gaining ground. I swerved sideways to avoid a fishing boat that had suddenly appeared from the shadows. This manoeuvre, together with some sudden wash from a speedboat that had cut in behind me, destabilised me. Desperately I struggled to gain control, but the jet ski bucked and twisted, colliding with the edge of a fishing net which was being hauled in behind the boat. I pitched headfirst into the icy-cold water!

Despite the weight of my backpack, I surfaced quickly. I didn't want to be struck by the circling jet ski. As I dived to avoid it, I became hopelessly entangled, caught up in the net that was being dragged up from the bottom of the harbour! Together with the mob of swirling fish, I was turned upside down and dragged further underwater.

I held my breath. My ears rang with the sound of the winch motor as it hauled in the catch. The net tightened around me. Sharp fins and spikes scratched my skin, but the more I shifted, the tighter the net became. My face was being cut to pieces by the thrashing fish as they pressed around me.

Tighter and tighter the net crushed around me. I struggled to reach the surface, but it was impossible. I couldn't hold my breath much longer.

I'd found the Ormond Jewel but now I was going to lose my life.

It had all been for nothing.

Like a desperate dolphin hopelessly entangled in a driftnet, I would drown.

CONSPIRACY 365

12 BOOKS 12 MONTHS

❑ BOOK 1

❑ BOOK 2

❑ BOOK 3

❑ BOOK 4

❑ BOOK 5

❑ BOOK 6

❑ BOOK 7

❑ BOOK 8

❑ BOOK 9

❑ BOOK 10

❑ BOOK 11

☑ GOT IT!

COLLECT ALL 12 BOOKS